Designing Data Products

The Data Products Series
Volume 1

Mario Meir-Huber

Technics Publications
SEDONA, ARIZONA

TECHNICS PUBLICATIONS

115 Linda Vista, Sedona, AZ 86336 USA
https://www.TechnicsPub.com

Edited by Steve Hoberman
Cover design by Lorena Molinari

First Printing 2025

Copyright © 2025 by Mario Meir-Huber

ISBN, print ed.   9798898160401
ISBN, Kindle ed.   9798898160418
ISBN, PDF ed.   9798898160425

To Elisabeth, for your endless support.
And to my lovely kids Helena, Vincent, and Clemens,
for forgiving the many hours I spent writing instead of playing.

Contents

Introduction

This book is for everyone who wants to understand what Data Products are, without getting lost in technical jargon. If you've heard the term but never quite knew what it means, this book is for you. It's written for beginners and curious minds who want to see how Data Products connect business and technology in a simple, understandable way.

This book contains three parts:

- Part 1 explains the idea and core principles of Data Products: what they are, what they aren't, and why they matter. We also introduce several easy-to-remember frameworks that keep the complexity of Data Products understandable.

- Part 2 looks at the business side, showing how Data Products create value and why they require more than just technology. This topic is often quite challenging to bring across for tech people, and serves as an introduction on how you can master the business discussion around Data Products.

- Part 3 turns to the technical side, offering an easy-to-grasp overview of how Data Products are built, managed, and scaled. We look at the most common patterns that you will encounter and need.

This book is not a deep technical manual or an advanced business playbook. You won't find complex algorithms or enterprise-level frameworks here. Instead, this book focuses on the essentials. Its purpose is to give you a clear and structured understanding of the topic and a language to confidently join the discussion around Data Products.

After reading this book, you'll understand what a Data Product is, why it exists, and how it brings value to organizations. You'll be able to recognize its key components, the roles involved, and the balance between business needs and technical design. Most importantly, you'll have the foundation to move forward.

Meeting Data Products

Part I lays the foundation for everything that follows. We'll dive into what Data Products are and what they are not. We'll discover the core traits that set great Data Products apart and explore the essential ingredients that make them work. This is where the journey begins: understanding the concept, defining the standards, and setting the stage for success.

ONE

Foundation

Seville, May 2024.

It was a beautiful spring day in this amazing Andalusian city. Warm sun, clear sky, and just the right amount of chaos in the streets. My wife and I were surrounded by old buildings with those typical southern Spanish facades: whitewashed walls, colorful tiles, balconies draped in flowers. Seville lives and breathes Flamenco and sometimes you'd catch it echoing from a hidden courtyard, other times from a guy strumming a guitar on the steps of a church.

There was a constant smell of tapas in the air, along with grilled seafood, garlic, and olive oil. The kind of scent that makes you hungry even if you just ate. We wandered without purpose, just walking, getting lost, and letting the city carry us. No schedule, no plans. It was the kind of place that makes you slow down without trying.

I was there with my wife on our honeymoon. And I really needed that pause. Back home, I was leading a large-scale data transformation program with 60 brilliant people, a tight timeline, and a serious budget. But for four days, I allowed myself to step out. My phone was in holiday mode. Mail notifications off. No Teams. Just the two of us, the city, and time.

That evening, we had picked out a little tapas bar we'd spotted earlier, tucked into a side street, full of locals. But, as every data executive knows, things rarely go as planned.

Later that afternoon, my phone lit up. The CTO was calling. On my honeymoon. Never a good sign.

I picked up. His voice was tense: the monthly reporting had failed. The algorithm that pulled our sales data from the warehouse and sent it to the owning company had stopped working. No numbers. No reports.

In a company listed on the stock market, that's not a glitch. It's a crisis. A single wrong number can shake investor trust. Millions, even billions, can vanish on paper in minutes. I didn't wait. I turned around, rushed back to the hotel, and got on the phone with my team. I needed to know what was going on.

It was chaos. No one had a clue what was going on. The algorithm had been running quietly for years until that specific day. No alerts, no documentation, and worst of all: no one on my current team even knew it existed. It turned out to be a legacy process, built long before any of us had joined. A ghost in the system, suddenly gone silent. We scrambled. Calls, emergency meetings, dead ends. Everyone was trying to piece together something they'd never seen before.

Finally, a developer who'd been with the company for over 15 years picked up. He knew the system. He knew the code. He pointed us in the right direction. Then, after what felt like hours, my data operations lead called. His voice was calm: "We've got it. It's under control."

Relief. I exhaled for the first time that afternoon. I closed my laptop, looked at my wife, and said: "Let's go find those tapas."

After my honeymoon, we held a debrief. The root cause? A single function in the data warehouse had been deprecated in the latest software upgrade. If people had known the job that failed, they could have reacted in time to this upgrade. If you work with data, this probably sounds familiar. And it's never just one thing. It's the lack of documentation. The missing context. The rushed "Data Products" that barely hold together.

This wasn't just a technical glitch. It was a symptom of something deeper: the hidden complexity that creeps into every organization that treats data as a second-class citizen. Over the years, I've seen these issues unfold repeatedly. I had sleepless nights, interrupted vacations, and firefights no one outside the team ever hears about. I've been in the trenches of data engineering, shoulder to shoulder with some of the smartest (and most sleep-deprived) people I know. And somewhere between broken pipelines and late-night calls, I made some of my closest friends.

The data world has seen its fair share of trends over the past decades, and I've been part of many of them. So why should we care about yet another buzzword: Data Products?

Because I don't see them as a buzzword at all. Data Products aren't a passing hype. They offer a pragmatic way to finally do things right. And while they're still in an emerging phase, recently even highlighted in Gartner's 2024 Hype Cycle,[1] they're not going away. It is quite the opposite: their relevance is growing fast.

Compared to other trends, Data Products have stayed under the radar. They're overshadowed by AI, even though they silently power it. Without good data, AI doesn't work, or worse, it works with full confidence on the wrong foundation until something breaks. Data Products provide the structure, quality, and clarity that AI desperately needs.

And that's not theory. Data Management is messy. I've lived through the chaos Data Products aim to fix. Over the past two decades, I've seen how things fall apart, not because of bad algorithms or poor infrastructure, but because of bad data. Broken pipelines. Conflicting definitions. Data models that don't match reality. Inaccuracies that nobody notices.

---

[1] Gartner: https://www.gartner.com/en/documents/5554195.

If any of that sounds familiar, then keep reading. This book is about how Data Products can bring order to the chaos. Data Products aren't a revolution like many trends before. They're a thoughtful evolution. They build on proven techniques, not hype. In this book, I'll show how to combine those techniques into a practical approach that works. Let's start by demystifying Data Products!

A paradigm shift in IT

Working with data often feels like playing a constant game of catch-up with IT, and it's one that data teams traditionally don't win.

First and foremost, data has always been methodologically behind classic IT. While many workloads moved to the cloud years ago, data workloads often remained stuck in on-premises environments. Enterprises were hesitant to move sensitive data to the cloud, and this hesitation left data teams operating under outdated conditions, while the rest of IT had already transitioned.

While IT teams were talking about microservices (small, independent applications each doing one job well and talking with each other to make the organization function smoothly), data teams were still building monoliths. Those big, old data warehouse servers had been around for years and weren't easily replaceable. And there wasn't even a trend pushing toward replacing them.

From data warehouses, we shifted to the next monolith: the data lake. It promised lower costs and better scalability, and in many cases, it failed to deliver. Today, most of those data lakes are being replaced by cloud-native tools.

While software engineers run automated builds, unit tests, and containerized deployments in seconds, most data teams are debugging broken ETL jobs by digging through email chains and outdated documentation. Imagine every software team implementing its own version of a login function. That's what we've done with data transformations for years. No standards, no common ingestion strategy. In large enterprises, data transformations are often pure chaos.

In contrast to classic software engineering, which has long relied on quality standards, testing, and architectural principles, data projects often lacked structure. Data was stored somewhere, somehow, simply because it had to be. The phrase "we just need to store it" was common. Clear quality standards, governance, and repeatable practices? Largely absent.

And we haven't even touched on the organizational side yet. Agile methods were well established in most modern software teams, but data teams? They continued working in waterfall mode. A strict design phase that lasted for months was followed by an even longer implementation phase.

The result? By the time the project went live, everything was already outdated. Business units were frustrated. With long release cycles and overloaded data teams, business units created their own solutions. Either with external solution providers or from scratch – often with Excel. More silos were created and there was no chance to keep up with the pace. Once a Silo was finally removed, two new ones were created.

Decentralization to solve the issues

In recent years, a strong trend toward decentralization has emerged. This wasn't surprising. After all, the centralization of data over the last decade(s) failed to solve the core problems. With modern approaches like Data Mesh[2] and Data Fabric (similar to microservices in that well-architected small applications simulate a well-integrated seamless system), the industry swung to full-scale decentralization. The thinking was: "If we can't control it, let's embrace it."

Technical teams felt relieved. The burden of data management was no longer solely on their shoulders. Business units welcomed the change, too, as there were no more rigid architectural guidelines preventing them from implementing what they needed. Distributed ownership of data? Sounds like a great idea. Business stakeholders were now responsible for data issues, not the technical teams.

---

[2] Dehghani: https://martinfowler.com/articles/data-monolith-to-mesh.html.

But then reality kicked in. What initially looked like a smart solution ended up shifting the problems rather than solving them. Instead of centralized data problems, we now had decentralized data problems. In many cases, decentralization was treated as a silver bullet, without acknowledging the organizational maturity needed to make it work. Ownership was handed over without building the capabilities to handle it. Business units were expected to manage data quality, documentation, and lifecycle decisions, but lacked the skills, resources, or incentives to do so. What was framed as empowerment often turned into abandonment. And when things went wrong, everyone pointed fingers, but no one truly owned the problem.

Hello, Data Products

Full-scale decentralization often forces a binary view: you're either centralized or decentralized. It starts to resemble a political debate. If you're not left, you're right; if you're not right, you're left. But real-world data challenges live in the grey zones between extremes. And that's where Data Products come in: they embrace that nuance.

The term Data Products is often associated with the Data Mesh, where it appears as "Data as a Product", and with the Data Fabric, where it's also referenced similarly. Both concepts treat Data Products as components of their broader frameworks. But I argue otherwise: Data Products stand on their own. I don't see them as merely a part of either.

Data Products, as defined in this book, take a lot of proven concepts from the old world and combine them with the new concepts from data mesh and data fabric. Data Products are more practical, and companies have the benefit of moving gradually to better data handling rather than re-inventing what was there. Data Products focus on the business problem, tackle the organization, and move away from technical silos. The outcome of a Data Product might be a report, an API, or an AI algorithm. We don't treat the lifecycle as a siloed approach; the Data Product approach ensures that we think end-to-end and build in quality into every step of it.

I've seen many definitions of data products. I prefer a simple one:

A data product delivers value to its consumers.

We don't need a complex definition. We need a usable one. A data product without quality doesn't deliver value. If it's unreliable, it doesn't deliver value. If it creates no strategic or financial impact, it doesn't deliver value either. So keep the definition simple: focus on value, and the right behaviors follow. And it's short enough to remember.

In the next section, we will examine all the key principles that make up great products – and will apply this to Data Products.

What are the key principles for Data Products?

This chapter is about Data Products. But to understand what a Data Product truly is, we first need to zoom out and take a closer look at the term product itself. Without a clear understanding of what makes something a product, it's easy to get lost in vague definitions when we apply the term to data.

Products are everywhere. Everyone consumes them, uses them, and interacts with them daily. Think of your phone, a coffee machine, or the streaming service you use. They all solve a specific problem for you.

So before diving into Data Products specifically, let's start by asking: What exactly is a product?

Interestingly, different people describe products in different ways, depending on their background or role. A designer might focus on usability, a businessperson on value, and an engineer on functionality.

To explore this further, let's examine this image:

What we see here is a car. Most people would immediately recognize it as a product: it's tangible, complete, and delivers clear value to its user. But now look at the next image.

What exactly can we see here? These are brake pads. Some might argue that this isn't really a product; it's just a component, part of the car we looked at earlier. But for others, brake pads are very much a product.

Car manufacturers buy them from specialized suppliers. Mechanics replace them as individual parts. Even you, as a car owner, might buy brake pads when maintenance is due. It's fair to say: brake pads are a product in their own right.

This brings us to an important nuance: products can contain other products. Not everything that is built or delivered is perceived as a full, standalone product. The context matters.

And that distinction becomes especially relevant when we talk about Data Products. Are we looking at a finished solution, or just a component? Data Products might be composed of different other Data Products, where each Data Product serves a dedicated purpose. Refinement is done within this process. Let's continue with our product images:

This is raw material. Iron, straight from the source. But even this is a product, isn't it? Car manufacturers, as well as the companies producing brake pads, use it. But they don't mine it themselves. They source it from suppliers. So, for them, it's also a product, however, not in its raw form. They need it already processed and usable for their specific purpose. Another ingredient of a product is that it goes through some form of processing. A product isn't useful for others who consume it if it isn't enriched in some way.

But does the story end with the car? Is that really the final product? Not quite.

The car might be the finished product for the manufacturer, but for a taxi company, it's a resource to offer a transportation service. For a ride-hailing app, it's part of a broader mobility platform. And for the end customer, it's a means to get from A to B. Even the car becomes part of something bigger. Products are nested, reused, and recombined. Products can be offered as a service.

But I'll stop here. I think you get the point: a product comes in many different flavors and definitions. And most importantly, only makes sense if it creates value for a specific group of people. Otherwise, it will quickly reach the end of its lifecycle.

The same should apply to Data Products.

While it's obvious what constitutes a product in the physical world, you might still have a lot of question marks when it comes to data. What exactly is a Data Product?

We've already introduced a definition, but let's now explore what a Data Product is, and also what it isn't. Let's have a look at a few real-world examples.

One of the most common questions I get is whether a table or a schema in a database qualifies as a Data Product. My answer is clear: no. It's like raw iron that may eventually become a car, but in its current form, it's just a data asset. Without refinement, it lacks the qualities we expect, such as reliability, usability, and business value.

What about a dashboard? In theory, a dashboard could fulfill many of the requirements of a Data Product. But in practice, most dashboards fall short. They often lack ownership, clear quality standards, or proper lifecycle management. The same holds for APIs: yes, an API can be a Data Product, but only if it adheres to clear standards and delivers value to defined users.

And an ML algorithm? It too can be delivered as a Data Product, for example, as a churn prediction model embedded in a CRM system.

As you can see, Data Products can take many forms. But simply transforming data and exposing it as a dataset in a database is not enough. A true Data Product must go through a defined process, meet specific requirements, and deliver sustained value. A dashboard is not a Data Product. An API neither, nor an AI algorithm. But Data Products can surface as them. That's what we'll explore in the next section.

The two dimensions of Data Products

A Data Product has two key dimensions: a **business** dimension and a **technical** dimension. To succeed, both must work together.

I've often been in discussions where the business side claimed that technology "just doesn't get it". Vice versa, the tech side said the same about business. That tension is part of the complexity of working with data, and Data Products are no exception.

From a business perspective, a Data Product only makes sense if it creates value for specific users. From a technical perspective, it must go through a defined engineering process, just like any other product.

The business dimension of Data Products

In general, people don't buy things unless they serve a purpose. The same should apply to Data Products. A great Data Product must be highly relevant to a specific group of people. Whether it's a dashboard used in board meetings to steer the company, or an algorithm that predicts customer churn for service teams. Both deliver value by serving a clear purpose.

Consequently, Data Products that are rarely used should be discontinued. I've seen many companies with hundreds of reports, but a large number of them are no longer used. I call these *Data Product antiques.*

So, the first important business aspect of a Data Product is:

Clear purpose and consumer relevance.

Some products are widely adopted, while others barely get used. A car, for example, is easy to use. Its design has followed the same principles for decades: a steering wheel, pedals, indicators, a horn, and a few other controls. Everyone knows how to operate it.

Good Data Products are just as intuitive within their intended domain. Great Data Products go beyond that. They're so usable that people outside the core audience can benefit from them, too.

Before Apple introduced the iPhone, smartphones already existed, mostly in the form of Windows CE devices. But very few people used them. They were complicated, hard to navigate, and required a lot of time to get started. This brings us to the next aspect of Data Products:

Usability and readiness

You can build the best Data Product, but if no one knows it exists, all that effort is wasted. A Data Product must be easy to discover and access, regardless of whether they are built in a centralized or decentralized way.

It also needs to be transparent about what it is and what it does. That means having a clear description, including its purpose, content, and how it should be used.

I once saw a customer dataset in a company that was widely shared. But there were no details on how customers were counted: gross, net, including churn or not? There was no owner listed, no update frequency documented, and no explanation of key filters. Different teams used it differently and came to conflicting conclusions. Eventually, trust eroded, and people started rebuilding their own versions. The two conflicting versions ended up in major discussions, even in the boardroom. The question was about what data is now correct. The original dataset counted customers by the end of the month, and the other one by the highest number during the month.

So, another important aspect of a Data Product is:

Reliability and transparency

Trust erodes, and wrong data can result in wrong decisions. Therefore, a Data Product must be reliable and transparent. Both are similar, but require different technical and organizational measures, which we will learn in the next chapters.

Most business users still find it extremely challenging to work with data. They often ask technical teams to "pull" the data they need, only to analyze it in Excel once again. We already touched on usability, but there's another critical dimension: making data understandable.

Several aspects contribute to this. It all starts with a clear description of what the Data Product is about and what data it contains, how it is calculated, and what users can do with it. Wherever possible, individual fields should be self-explanatory, with well-defined meanings. KPIs must be clearly defined, and business terms should be explained in plain language.

This level of clarity removes hesitation and lowers the barrier for business users to confidently work with Data Products.

This brings us to the next aspect of a Data Product:

Understandable and self-describing

When business users don't understand the data, they'll always ask for a "data dump" they can make sense of.

Data Products need to be trusted. This has always been important for dashboards, but it's even more critical for AI. When someone reviews a dashboard and spots flawed data, it can be flagged and corrected. But AI consumes whatever data it's given, and it doesn't ask questions.

That's why every Data Product must have a clear owner. Someone who feels accountable for its quality and relevance. There must be mechanisms in place to ensure the data stays up to date. No one wants to work with data that's outdated or disconnected from business reality. Like any traditional product, a Data Product requires lifecycle management. When it becomes irrelevant, it needs a refresh. Ultimately, it should be retired entirely. This means that there must be an approval process – when to bring a Data Product into production and when to retire it.

Just walk into any large enterprise. You'll likely hear about the countless dashboards in their BI tools and the Excel reports being emailed around. And yet, no one really knows which ones are still relevant, because no one is managing them.

This brings us to the last business aspect of a Data Product:

Approved and up to date

Ensure that your Data Products are actively managed throughout their lifecycle and accurately reflect the current state of the business. Otherwise, they become ghost assets within the system.

The technical dimension of Data Products

We already looked at the car as a product in the previous section. Let's build on that example to highlight another key aspect of Data Products. Just like a car is made up of many other products, such as brake pads, sensors, or tires, a Data Product can also be composed of multiple other Data Products.

Let's take a closer look at a sales dashboard. This dashboard might rely on multiple Data Products: for example, one containing customer sales data, another based on a market prediction algorithm, and perhaps even one incorporating competitive intelligence. Each of these could exist as an independent Data Product.

When Data Products are built on top of other Data Products, interoperability becomes a critical challenge. If each Data Product follows its own standard (or no standard at all), composability breaks down. Without shared definitions and consistent structures, Data Products can't be reliably combined or reused.

Consequently, the next important aspects of Data Products are:

Composable and Interoperable

Without composability, Data Products become isolated assets which limit their impact and reusability.

Data Products form the foundation for company-wide decision-making. Sales Data Products are used to incentivize sellers. Customer Data Products help calculate churn risk. But if these Data Products are not trustworthy, errors occur. These errors lead to poor or wrong decisions. Regardless of their purpose, every Data Product must be reliable and contain accurate data.

Security is just as essential. Data Products often power critical business processes and may contain sensitive information. If such a product is exposed to the public when it shouldn't be, the consequences are serious. It creates pressure on both business and data teams. This can damage the credibility of the entire organization.

Therefore, Data Products must be:

Trustworthy, secure, and reliable

Data Products that lack security, reliability, or trust will ultimately fail, regardless of how well they are designed.

Imagine a company with a perfectly designed product, but in the end, no one buys it. This has happened many times throughout economic history. One example is Super Video versus VHS: although Super Video was technically superior, VHS was marketed far more effectively.

The same applies to Data Products. A Data Product that no one can find will ultimately go unused. It must be discoverable, both for business and technical users, ideally through a well-managed asset catalog.

But discovery alone is not enough. Once a Data Product has been found, it must also be usable. Imagine having a fully documented, well-managed catalog, but no way to actually access the data. It's like dangling a carrot in front of someone: the value is visible, but unreachable. A Data Product must therefore be technically addressable and ready for consumption.

The next important aspect of a Data Product is:

Discoverable and addressable

Without proper discoverability and technical access, Data Products remain invisible and unused, regardless of their potential value.

Let's look at what successful companies do: they build their products in a modular way, using pre-built platforms. Returning to the car manufacturing example, battery packs are often built on common platforms and then reused across different models. But this isn't unique to the automotive industry. Apple follows a similar approach by developing reusable components across its product lines.

This strategy significantly increases economies of scale and reduces overall costs. It also enables these companies to specialize by making the core components that power their main products more efficient. And importantly, it avoids reinventing the wheel each time.

However, one critical question often comes up: what comes first, the platform or the product? In my experience, it's both. A new product often triggers enhancements to the platform, which then benefit future products as well.

The same logic applies to Data Products. Technical platforms and data models should be shared to maximize efficiency and foster reuse. There shouldn't be competing ingestion routes or multiple data models representing the same entity. While this may seem counter to the trend of decentralization, it's essential to ensure consistency and maintain data quality.

Therefore, the next aspect of Data Products is:

Shared platform and models

With shared platforms and models, teams avoid constantly reinventing the wheel.

Data pipelines break. Data sources get corrupted. I've seen all of it.

Now imagine applying this to a car manufacturer: if your car constantly breaks down, at some point you'll abandon it or replace it altogether. A good product must be reliable: able to deliver what's needed, when it's needed. The same applies to Data

Products: they must be built with a level of robustness that can handle the failure of individual components.

Because Data Products are often composed of other Data Products, each one must be reliable enough not to break others. And if a dependent Data Product fails, this scenario must be accounted for since it's not an exception; it's part of reality.

In the past, many data solutions were built ad hoc and with minimal engineering discipline. Business pressure often led to shortcuts in design and delivery, which came at the expense of long-term robustness.

As a result, today's Data Products must be:

Robust

Imagine stepping into a car with no seatbelts. The last time it was serviced? Unknown. Airbags? Not even installed. Would you go on a trip in that car? I wouldn't.

Decades ago, that kind of setup was normal. But after enough accidents, regulators stepped in. Seatbelts became mandatory and saved countless lives. Airbags followed a similar path. They became standard after people recognized their value.

The same applies to Data Products. And yet, when we look at many of the Data Products used in practice today, it often feels like we're driving without seatbelts or airbags. We're still at a very early stage. There's a strange normalcy around poor data quality: it's accepted, even when it clearly wouldn't be tolerated elsewhere.

Data quality is a first-class citizen in the world of Data Products. It's the seatbelt and airbag that ensure safety, integrity, and reliability.

This brings us to another key aspect of Data Products:

Data quality and integrity management

Data Products without quality aren't products. They're liabilities.

In complex systems like Data Products, things will eventually go wrong. It's inevitable. When they do, it's essential to understand why. Identifying the root cause allows teams to prevent similar issues in the future through structured analysis and targeted improvements.

This requires proactive monitoring and alerting to detect issues early and respond before they escalate.

Therefore, another aspect of Data Products is:

Monitoring and observability

Unmonitored Data Products are a risk to the business. They are like a ticking time bomb waiting to go off.

Data Products versus data assets versus data projects

An important question to raise is how Data Products differ from other, seemingly similar concepts, such as data assets and data projects. While there are overlaps, the differences are essential. Let's break them down.

Data assets

A data asset refers to data in its raw or semi-structured form. It may contain valuable information, but it doesn't yet serve a specific business purpose. Data assets are typically not managed with the same level of ownership, lifecycle, or usability in mind as Data Products. They often reside within specific teams and are focused on data storage rather than value delivery.

In contrast, a Data Product is designed to meet concrete business needs. It may consist of multiple data assets, but only when those assets are properly managed, productized, and enriched with the characteristics we've previously outlined.

Data projects

A data project is typically goal-oriented, time-bound, and designed to answer a specific business question or solve a defined problem. It has a clear start and end point. The focus is often on one-time analysis or building a prototype.

A Data Product, on the other hand, is ongoing. It is continuously managed, maintained, and improved. While a data project might evolve into a Data Product, the two differ in intent, scope, and sustainability. You don't build a car to use it once – it should serve you for many years.

Key learnings

- **Data chaos is real**: legacy issues, missing ownership, lack of quality – all that lead to challenges in how we deal with data today.

- **What a Data Product is**: we defined the term and derived key characteristics from successful products.

- **Data Products bring value**: value to its users and the company. This value can also be monetary.

- **The two dimensions of Data Products**: we looked at both dimensions of Data Products, business and technology, and examined the key characteristics.

- **Data Products are more than just data**: data assets are raw. Data projects are temporary. Data Products are managed, value-driven, and enduring.

Two

GAP

5 a.m. It was another sleepless night.

Working across three time zones was tough: our engineering team in Mumbai and management on the U.S. West Coast. Me, in Vienna, Central Europe. A 12-hour span I had to bridge. The project I had taken on in my new role was exciting, but equally challenging. For weeks, we made no progress. We simply couldn't get the Hadoop cluster deployed for the customer.

Our client, a large bank, was both innovative and impatient. They wanted to move to the next level of data management using cutting-edge technology. I quickly built a good relationship with the CDO. We shared the same mindset and drive for innovation.

But this night was critical. The customer had set a final deadline: the system had to be running by midday the next day. I worked with the engineering team through the night to troubleshoot and resolve the issue. After hours of debugging, they deployed the fix. I watched the status screen, waiting.

Finally, at 5:10 a.m., the status flipped from *"provisioning"* to *"running."* I wanted to jump and shout, but my daughter was sleeping, and I was too exhausted. I just wrote an email to the customer: "It works." Then I collapsed into bed.

This was a purely technical problem, and back at the time, I believed that the only challenges in data work were purely technical. I was so wrong. Technology, in fact, is only one aspect; there are two other important ingredients that we will learn about in this chapter.

The GAP Triad

In this chapter, we'll look at the three core ingredients that shape every step of working with data. I call it the GAP. Not a gap to close, but a triad: Governance, Architecture, and People. This framework is essential for the following chapters, and they are the solid foundation we will now learn before we have a look at the Data Products process in Chapter 3.

All three dimensions, Governance, Architecture, and People, are essential at every step of building successful Data Products.

- Governance ensures quality, trust, and compliance.

- Architecture provides the technical backbone for robustness and scalability.

- People and Culture drive adoption, change management, and continuous improvement.

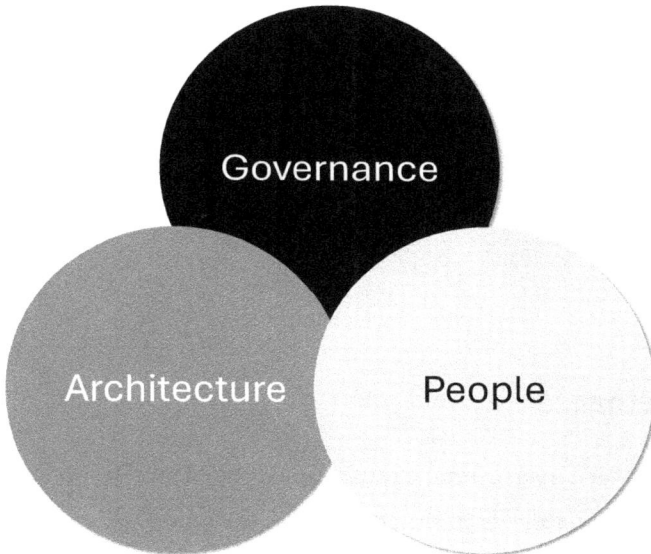

Figure 1: The Triad for Data Products.

In many data transformation programs I've seen, these three areas were treated as separate tracks. Poorly aligned, or only loosely connected to the core initiative. They progressed at different speeds, creating friction. Change Management programs raised expectations that the platform couldn't meet. Governance frameworks existed only on paper, disconnected from delivery. Technical implementations moved forward without real engagement from users.

You won't find a general introduction to data governance or change management here; we will talk about each of these topics while we gradually progress in the next chapters and volumes of the book series. Instead, this chapter takes a pragmatic view: showing how governance, architecture, and people must be embedded into the process of building Data Products instead of treating them as standalone disciplines.

The goal is not complexity. It's integration and making these three forces work together to deliver real outcomes through Data Products.

Governance

Data governance is important for qualitative Data Products. Every Data Product needs it. But dare to ask for a budget, and your job might be at risk. I've heard plenty of senior leaders say things like, "We don't need data governance." This is a misperception, as on the first look, it doesn't bring business value. In fact, it is a very important ingredient to build great Data Products. Investments in data governance don't pay off initially – but the results of not doing so will surface over the years to come.

So, how do we deal with the long-standing denial of data governance in organizations?

Simply not talking about it.

Instead, we take quality for granted. We talk about building high-quality Data Products. We avoid using the term "data governance" because it often triggers resistance that stems from failed data governance initiatives in the past. But in practice, when building Data Products, governance is integrated into every step. It's not a separate discipline. It's embedded in the process itself. We'll explore how this works in Chapter 3.

Governance must also be pragmatic and problem-solving. Most governance programs I've seen are disproportionate, over-engineered, and never make it beyond PowerPoint slides. They involve too many people, rely on overly complex processes, and result in endless meetings with no real outcomes.

Let's examine the definition of Data Products again:

A data product delivers value to its consumers.

A Data Product without quality doesn't deliver value. There is no discussion needed about that. If it is of bad quality, nobody will use the Data Product, thus removing all value.

The business dimension of data governance

Data governance delivers major benefits for business use. It is essential for building trust in your Data Products, especially when exposing them to internal or external users.

However, not every key principle introduced in Chapter one is equally relevant in this context. For Data Products, three key aspects stand out: usability and readiness, reliability and transparency, and understandable and self-describing.

Usability and readiness

With a car, you know exactly how to operate it – it's common sense. The same applies to modern smartphones: they're easy to use by design. Data Products should follow the same principle. There should not be a need for complex onboarding, but the Data Product should be self-service and clearly described for end-user usability.

Take Google Analytics as an example. Most users know how to navigate the platform and find what they need. Why? Because it's designed with usability in mind. However, only a small number of Data Products are delivered as Dashboards, but usability is a much broader term and needs to be adjusted to the target users.

In contrast, some data assets are hidden deep inside databases, undocumented and hard to access. But if a Data Product can't be found or understood, I wouldn't call it a Data Product at all. A usable Data Product is clearly described – ideally in a data catalog.

As business users begin working with more Data Products, consistent terminology and naming conventions become essential. They dramatically improve usability by making key elements easier to recognize and interpret. This reduces cognitive friction and enables faster adoption.

Reliability and transparency

Business users need to understand how reliable a Data Product is. Their first questions are often: Is this correct? Why is the data shown this way? What are the quality standards behind it?

Data governance helps answer these questions by defining clear KPIs and quality benchmarks. It also ensures transparency around how the data was created and how it evolved throughout the processing pipeline (a topic we'll cover in more detail in Chapter 3).

When working with a Data Product, business users want to understand the origin of the data. They need to trust it and clarity helps improve this trust. Sending them into a maze of complex SQL transformations only creates confusion.

Modern data governance tools support this need with built-in data lineage visualizations, helping users see where the data comes from and how it has been transformed.

Understandable and self-describing

Here we find a key differentiator of Data Products: understandability. When a Data Product is easy to interpret, whether by business users or AI systems, it creates significant value. It shortens time to market, reduces silos, and minimizes friction across teams.

Clear Data Products also reduce the number of alignment meetings. Why? Because users instantly understand what they're working with. A well-described Data Product speaks for itself. In reporting, this means visuals are clearly labeled and contextualized. In datasets, it means columns are named clearly, calculations are documented, and KPIs are explicitly defined.

Another essential component is "data about the data", which is also known as metadata. Metadata helps users understand what to expect. Imagine opening a Data Product and seeing a field called "fname". What does it mean? First name? Full name? Something else? A metadata repository can remove this ambiguity by making such definitions clear and accessible. A good Metadata description would be: "fname – This field stores the full name of a customer. It starts with the first name, followed by the middle name (optional), and ends with the last name in the format "[Firstname] – [Middle name (optional)] – [Last name]". This not only improves readability for humans, but also gives an edge for AI processing this data.

The technical dimension of data governance

Data governance requires a lot of technical engineering work. This is why most key aspects defined in Chapter one are relevant for data governance. It's also why many aspects of a well-designed Data Product are derived from effective data governance.

Composable and interoperable

Interoperability is achieved in Data Products when they are clearly described and built on shared standards. These standards can vary from REST for APIs, to Data Contracts, to Dataspaces for structured exposure.

Composability is the natural outcome of interoperability, but it breaks down when interoperability is missing.

Governance plays a key role here by enforcing standards, naming conventions, and shared contracts that make interoperability possible at scale.

Trustworthy, secure, and reliable

A Data Product must be reliable not just in how it operates, but in the integrity of the data it contains. One key goal is to provide transparency: where the data originated, how it was transformed, and why those transformations were applied. This level of insight helps build trust and ensures ongoing reliability.

Security is another critical dimension. It is typically enforced through encryption, access controls, and governance policies. Common techniques include row- and column-level security as well as role-based access controls (RBAC). This ensures that users only see the data relevant to them.

A reliable Data Product should also have clear error-handling and fallback strategies, especially when upstream dependencies fail.

Discoverable and addressable

Data Products that can't be found by users are useless. No one will use them. Data governance plays a key role in solving this, primarily through tools like data catalogs or Data Product repositories that make products easier to find and understand.

But discoverability and addressability go beyond simply listing a product somewhere. It's equally important to provide clear APIs, access rules, and documentation that make the product usable in practice.

The ideal scenario? Data Products are made available to consumers via self-service, enabled with a rock-solid data governance embedded into the platform.

Robust

The robustness of a Data Product is just as important as the robustness of any other IT system. It's a technical discipline that relies on thorough testing and well-defined quality measures. While robustness is often seen as an architectural concern, it also depends heavily on data governance. This provides the guardrails needed to ensure stability and consistency.

Typical practices that support robustness include data contracts and testing. From a governance perspective, data contracts are especially relevant, as they define clear expectations between producers and consumers of data.

Data Quality and Integrity Management

Data Quality is one of the most critical aspects of data governance. Governance frameworks define the guardrails and guidelines for how quality is measured, monitored, and maintained.

When issues arise, alerting mechanisms can surface problems early, allowing Data Product teams to act before they impact consumers.

Modern Data Quality tools also offer data lineage and anomaly detection, helping teams trace the flow of data through pipelines and identify deviations from expected patterns. Together, these capabilities are essential for ensuring that Data Products remain trustworthy and of high quality.

Architecture

The second foundational aspect of Data Products is architecture. Some might argue that this is the core domain. In fact, in many organizations, it's treated that way. I've seen countless data sets managed purely as engineering tasks. But while engineering is essential, it's only one of the three pillars that make up a successful Data Product.

There are many differing views on what Data Architecture really means. In many cases, teams simply assemble a few tools for data processing and label it a "data architecture."

In this book, we'll take a more complete approach. It is driven by a process, not just by technology choices. The form of architecture just mentioned in the previous paragraph, the tooling layer, is only one step in a broader process. Data always follows a lifecycle, and this is why we'll explore multiple architectural angles throughout this book.

The full process will be introduced in Chapter 3. It goes beyond tooling to focus on how data is integrated, delivered, and ultimately transformed into business value.

In the section you're reading now, we'll look at how a solid architectural foundation contributes to the success of Data Products.

As expected, many of the following aspects fall within the technical dimension. In the next sections, we'll explore each of them in detail. We will focus on how they contribute to building robust and effective Data Products.

Technical reliability is achieved through various mechanisms, such as fault tolerance, failure recovery, and integrated data lineage. While data quality is often addressed through governance, it must also be enforced by technically sound implementations.

A complete Data Product, from a technical perspective, includes everything required for actual use, such as well-defined access mechanisms, APIs, and interfaces. In Chapter 1, we introduced the concept of reusability. This becomes possible when Data Products expose clear APIs and are accompanied by proper documentation and descriptions.

To fully manage a Data Product, it's not enough to define ownership and processes; they also need to be implemented in the technical layer.

The business dimension of Architecture

While the architectural dimension is largely driven by technical implementations, it serves as a critical foundation for all business-facing aspects of a Data Product. Without a solid technical base, even the best-designed Data Product will ultimately fail.

Within the business dimension of architecture, one aspect stands out: ensuring that Data Products remain approved and up to date over time.

Approved and up to date

While approving a Data Product is primarily a matter of ownership and lifecycle, which is often driven by people and processes, it also has a significant technical dimension. It requires thoughtful engineering, close alignment with business needs, and clear planning to ensure the product is sustainable.

The second dimension, keeping Data Products up to date, relies on a range of engineering techniques. One key aspect is understanding the required update frequency: some Data Products must support real-time or near-real-time data, while others may only need hourly or daily refresh cycles. The architectural design must reflect these needs to ensure reliability and relevance.

The technical dimension of Architecture

Architecture is inherently technology-driven, so it's no surprise that many aspects of Data Products are anchored in the technical dimension. A well-designed architecture not only supports the core principles of Data Products but also ensures they remain economically viable at scale.

While we haven't yet explored the cost dimension in detail, it's important to note that sound architectural decisions significantly reduce the long-term cost of running Data Products. This connection between technical excellence and cost efficiency will be addressed in Chapter 3, when we introduce the Data Product development process.

Composable and interoperable

We introduced reusability as a core principle of Data Products. This is closely tied to their composability and interoperability. To enable reusability, Data Products must expose well-defined interfaces, such as APIs, that allow them to be integrated and built upon by other products.

However, reusability also depends on other qualities like robustness. A reusable Data Product must not only perform reliably on its own but must also avoid breaking others or being broken by others when used in combination.

Composability and interoperability are typically achieved through standards and clear documentation. The most advanced form of this is Data Sharing via Data Spaces. This is a decentralized model where data remains under the control of the original owner while still being accessible for reuse by participating parties.

Trustworthy, secure, and reliable

A Data Product that cannot be trusted will not survive long. Reliability is a core discipline of Data Product engineering and requires a broad set of practices. Well-designed Data Products are rigorously tested. It starts with unit tests, but also incorporates more advanced techniques to validate business logic and algorithmic correctness as part of the process. In addition, pipeline monitoring and transparency in data transformation are essential to ensure consistent and traceable outputs.

Security is equally critical. A Data Product must be protected against unauthorized access. This happens not just through encryption and access rights, but by enforcing data minimization principles. The "need-to-know" principle ensures that users can only access the data required for their specific role or use case. This is implemented through mechanisms like role-based access control, row- and column-level security, and data masking.

Shared platform and models

This aspect clearly sets architecture apart from governance and people. A shared technical platform and standardized data models significantly increase both the speed and quality of Data Product development. While not every Data Product requires a shared foundation, many do, especially in enterprise environments where consistency, efficiency, and reuse matter. Like how car manufacturers reuse engine platforms across different models, shared infrastructure in data environments leads to greater agility and reduced costs.

To develop such a shared platform, it is essential to define a target architecture. This includes a unified strategy for data ingestion, standardized tools for data transformation, and common governance mechanisms. We will explore these architectural components in Chapter six and go deeper into platform tooling in the second volume of this book. The same logic applies to shared data models, which we will examine in Chapter 7, along with different modeling strategies that support Data Product scalability.

Robust

Robust Data Products are the result of solid engineering practices combined with clear governance rules. Robustness is critical because Data Products must handle failures, incorrect inputs, and unexpected parameters without breaking. They are designed for durability, and if they fail, they should fail gracefully, with minimal disruption to the end user. Recovery mechanisms should be transparent and automatic.

A key challenge with Data Products is that they always follow a defined process. Data passes through multiple transformation steps. Some of these steps are independent, while others are tightly coupled. If a single step in this sequence fails, it can compromise the entire Data Product. One proven technique to manage these dependencies is the use of Directed Acyclic Graphs (DAGs). DAGs help to clearly model the relationships and execution order between transformation steps. We will explore how DAGs support robust Data Product design in more detail in Chapter 6.

Achieving robustness requires a decoupled architecture and extensive testing of each component. Systems must be equipped to detect potential issues early and apply retry strategies where necessary. Finally, robustness also means defining and meeting Service Level Agreements (SLAs). This includes guarantees for uptime, refresh intervals, and response times. These expectations must be both measurable and enforced to build trust with consumers of the Data Product.

Monitoring and observability

Once Data Products are in production, they must be continuously monitored. This applies to the entire lifecycle: from the original data source to the point where the product delivers business value.

Data Products typically rely on multiple ingest pipelines and transformation steps. Given this complexity, failures are likely. Proactive monitoring helps detect issues early and enables teams to respond quickly or to learn from failures when they occur. Many modern data platforms offer built-in monitoring tools that show the status of each step in a pipeline. Dashboards can also visualize the operational health of a Data Product in real time.

Let's take a sales reporting Data Product as an example. If the nightly batch job that ingests ERP sales data fails silently, the dashboard may still display outdated numbers, without any visible indication of failure. Eventually, business users will sense that something is wrong and escalate the issue to the engineering team. At that point, it becomes awkward: the business rightfully questions the reliability of the solution, and IT is left in a reactive position. Worse still, if the issue goes unnoticed, critical decisions might be made based on stale data.

With proper monitoring and alerting, such as failure notifications or data freshness indicators embedded in the process, such issues can be identified early and addressed before they impact the business.

A Data Product is never static. Whether data flows in continuously or on scheduled intervals, monitoring and alerting are not optional. These techniques are essential to maintaining reliability and trust.

People

Everything scales or fails with people and culture. And the same holds true for Data Products. You can implement the best tools, platforms, and governance structures, but if people resist using them, the initiative will fail. That's why it's essential to address the human aspect in every Data Product initiative.

Business value can only be achieved when stakeholders are actively integrated into the process. This creates a clear intersection with how teams and stakeholders are managed across the organization.

Another critical aspect is ownership. This is a topic we'll explore in detail in Chapter 5. In the context of Data Products, ownership is often shared, which adds complexity but is essential for long-term success.

Nearly all core principles of Data Products are touched by people; there are countless points of intersection. Success depends on reducing resistance, convincing teams to work in new ways, and ensuring they are properly trained. Resistance often stems from fear of the unknown, which is why training and upskilling are critical. Removing that fear and clearly showing the benefits helps bring your Data Products to life.

Training also reinforces other principles, such as quality. Proper training benefits the quality of data in different ways.

Unlike the previous sections, I won't map the people dimension to each principle, because it is simply embedded in all of them. However, two stand out, and we'll take a closer look at them: Clear Purpose and Consumer Relevance, and Usability and Readiness.

Clear purpose and consumer relevance

Data Products must always be tailored to customer needs with no exceptions. A Data Product developed purely from an internal IT idea is rarely relevant or successful.

To align with customer expectations, it's essential to involve the customer from the very beginning. Ideally, the initial idea or request even comes from them. Several techniques help ensure that customer relevance stays at the core of the process. It starts with ideation workshops, where teams and stakeholders jointly define needs and priorities. This early alignment helps guarantee that the Data Product will deliver real value.

Throughout development, agile methodologies and cross-functional teams that include the customer are key to successful execution. Deep integration with business stakeholders ensures that feedback is continuous and that the product evolves in line with expectations.

Usability and readiness

Closely related to customer relevance is the principle of usability and readiness. Data Products that are easy to use, whether through well-designed APIs, intuitive dashboards, or accessible AI interfaces, deliver more value and gain broader adoption.

Achieving this requires continuous involvement from end users. Their feedback is essential to ensure the product doesn't drift away from its intended purpose. If a Data Product becomes too complex, it's necessary to simplify the interface, whether that means redesigning the API, improving the dashboard, or refining the user interaction model.

What's next?

The GAP triad, Governance, Architecture, and People, forms a critical foundation for successful Data Products. Together, they create a strong and interdependent framework that supports long-term value and sustainability.

In this chapter, we introduced these three dimensions at a high level. But there's much more to each of them. In the next chapter, we'll explore a practical framework that outlines the process of building and maintaining Data Products, from data retrieval to their usage.

At every step of that process, Governance, Architecture, and People must be thoughtfully and consistently integrated.

Key learnings

- **The triad for Data Products**: GAP, consisting of governance, architecture, and people.

- **Data Products are process-driven:** data flows through different transformations and comes from different pipelines, and is always in motion.

- **The GAP should be in every step:** only by this, high-quality Data Products are possible. The GAP is a key aspect every Data Product should follow.

- **The impact of GAP:** we discussed the impact of governance, architecture, and people towards the principles of Data Products.

THREE

DRIVE

I was deep in preparing a presentation for our upcoming data department restructuring. One of my main goals in the first month at the new company was to break free from the rigid waterfall setup I had inherited from my predecessor. Just as I was aligning the final slides, my phone rang. It was the Director of Controlling. His voice tense:

"Mario, could you join us urgently? I'm in a meeting with the CFO and CCO. We're debating the net adds and we need help."

I closed my laptop and headed straight to the executive floor. Five minutes later, I stepped into a room thick with tension. The Controlling Director quickly brought me up to speed: the Finance and Marketing departments were once again showing different numbers for net customer adds. He admitted this wasn't new; it happened nearly every month. The discrepancies were usually minor, but the finger-pointing never stopped.

I was stunned. Net customer adds are a fundamental metric. Surely that should be straightforward? But anyone who's worked with data knows it's rarely that simple.

I huddled with my team to get to the bottom of it. No one had deeply investigated it before. After all, the monthly net-add mismatch had somehow become an accepted ritual. But it didn't take long to uncover the root cause: each department was using a different pipeline with different definitions.

Controlling relied on a monthly batch job that simply compared the customer base at the end of each month. Marketing, on the other hand, used a real-time data stream developed by external consultants. And here's the twist: they counted every new contract, even if a customer canceled later that month. The churned customers weren't deducted. Same data domain. Different pipelines. Different logic. Different truth.

This one case revealed multiple architectural and governance issues:

- Competing ingest strategies (monthly batch versus real-time).
- Redundant integration of the same data with divergent semantics.
- No shared KPI definitions, or worse, no ownership of the truth.

What should have been a single, reliable Data Product had fragmented into two conflicting views.

What this story shows is more than a one-off mistake. It's a symptom of a deeper issue: the absence of a shared, repeatable process for creating and managing Data Products. Without such a framework, every team ends up building its own version of truth, leading to issues like the above one.

While the example of net customer adds wasn't developed as a Data Product, it shows the risk of repeating past mistakes: pulling data from the source, transforming it, and calculating KPIs. If all of this is done without alignment or synchronization, we won't fix issues but create new ones.

That's exactly what this chapter is about. We'll explore a process-driven framework that respects the nature of data. Data is always in motion. We will look at how to build, operate, and continuously improve Data Products in a structured way.

The DRIVE Framework for Data Products

I didn't choose the car metaphor by accident, as it carries through into this chapter. The framework we're about to explore is called DRIVE, and just like a car, it helps you "drive" your Data Products forward. Think of it as the assembly line. We get from the initial chassis to the full car in this process. And important – in every process step, there are several aspects of quality management necessary. Our Data Product process implements this as well – with the GAP triad.

The DRIVE Framework captures the core lifecycle of any Data Product, from **Data R**etrieval to **I**ntegration, and eventually how **V**alue is **E**xtracted out of it. If you've worked with data before, many of these steps will feel familiar because this framework is built on proven practices.

This chapter provides a high-level overview of the process every Data Product goes through. In the next sections, we'll explore each step and how it helps you build better, more reliable Data Products.

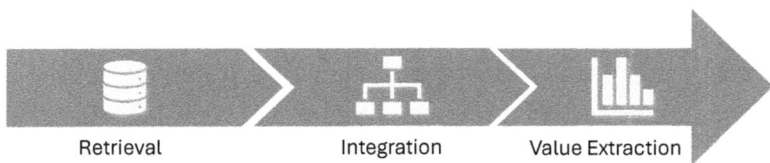

Figure 2: The DRIVE Framework: Data Retrieval, Integration, and Value Extraction.

Step 1: Data retrieval

The very first step for every Data Product is to retrieve the data it relies on. Before this can begin, it must be clearly defined which data is required and for what purpose. Data can come in various forms: structured, semi-structured, or unstructured, and in different formats such as JSON, plain text, or relational tables.

In complex enterprise environments, data is sourced from a wide range of systems, including CRM platforms, ERP systems, production systems, sensors, POS terminals, online services like

Google Analytics, or external providers. Integrating this data is rarely straightforward, as it involves handling technical complexity, inconsistent formats, and differing levels of data quality. These challenges must be addressed with careful planning and the right architecture to ensure a reliable foundation for the Data Product.

Retrieving data is the first and arguably most critical step in building a Data Product. Two core strategies are typically applied: real-time retrieval and batch processing. While real-time approaches offer the advantage of up-to-date data, they are also resource-intensive and require careful engineering. Batch processing, in contrast, is often more cost-efficient but introduces latency and complexity in handling data changes.

At this early stage, data quality is paramount. Errors introduced during acquisition will propagate downstream and affect every subsequent step. One important mechanism to safeguard quality is the use of Data Contracts. These are agreements between source and consumer systems that specify which data is delivered, in what format, and under what conditions. These contracts also serve as a foundation for collecting metadata and establishing data lineage. Data Contracts might be very restrictive (not letting corrupt data in), or they serve to improve data quality at data-producing systems.

To capture data changes efficiently in batch scenarios, Change Data Capture (CDC) techniques are commonly used. Instead of reloading entire datasets, CDC identifies and ingests only the changes since the last load. This preserves system resources and lowers costs. Real-time systems rely on event streams or outbox patterns to push change events directly to a landing zone. We will explore both techniques in Chapter 6.

Managing dependencies is another key challenge. Data Products often rely on multiple upstream sources, and their order of arrival can affect downstream transformations. To handle this complexity, many systems model dependencies using Directed Acyclic Graphs (DAGs), ensuring that processing steps execute in the correct sequence.

Numerous tools are involved in the retrieval phase, and while this book takes a tool-agnostic stance, we will reference selected technologies in later chapters to illustrate best practices and implementation strategies.

Figure 3 shows the typical flow of how data retrieval can be built (highly simplified). What we can see here is that in this sample, the POS Data needs to be integrated after the CRM and SAP data were transformed. These dependencies are managed via DAGs.

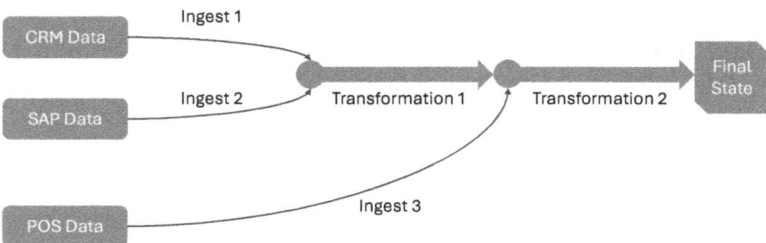

Figure 3: A DAG for data ingestion.

If you've worked in data for some time, this step may remind you of the classic E in the ETL or ELT process. And that's no coincidence. The DRIVE framework intentionally builds on established engineering practices, but it goes further. Traditional ETL/ELT processes are largely technical in nature, focusing on moving and transforming data. In contrast, Data Products demand a more holistic approach.

In the DRIVE model, this phase still includes technical architecture (as described in the GAP triad in Chapter 2) but also integrates Governance and People as equally critical dimensions. Data Products are not just about moving data. They must be of high quality. That means embedding data quality rules, defining ownership, and ensuring business alignment. All these aspects go way beyond the scope of classical ETL pipelines.

This is why Data Products deserve their own framework. They aren't simply outputs of a pipeline; they are managed, governed, and consumed assets that drive business value.

Once this first step is done, we have our first data assets ready for our Data Product. These data assets we will refer to as input ports, which is a common term in the language of Data Products. While we typically rely on high-quality data already in the input ports, we won't take this for granted in the very first step. All input ports need to be checked (either for each ingestion or periodically) against their corresponding data contracts.

Step 2: Integrating data

Once the data is retrieved from producing systems, the next step is integration. This is where raw data gets structured, transformed, and prepared for business use. Traditionally, data integration relied on data warehouses. Today, this approach remains relevant and is often complemented by modern cloud-based technologies.

In recent years, the emergence of big data has brought data lakes to the forefront. These environments handle large volumes and diverse formats of data. The lines between warehouses and lakes have since blurred, especially in modern cloud architectures. As a result, many organizations now adopt hybrid models that combine the strengths of both.

This phase is also the primary phase for transformation. While initial cleanup or parsing might happen during retrieval, most of the transformation, like reshaping, enriching, and aggregating, takes place here. Tools like SQL, Apache Spark, and dbt (Data Build Tool) are commonly used to manage and orchestrate this process.

We have different angles on how we can look at Data Products:

- **Source-aligned**: These Data Products heavily resemble the data as it comes from source systems. The data stays close to the source system structure and its purpose. A sample would be a Data Product that is aligned with the CRM system and exposes information about the customers.

- **Aggregated**: Data Products have some transformation logic applied. Different data-producing systems might contribute to this. A sample would be a Data Product that combines the CRM system with behavioral data about customers on the website.

- **Consumer-aligned**: Data Products are oriented to the consumer's needs rather than on how the data is produced in the source systems. A dashboard for Sales might need much more detail than just the data existing in our CRM. Different transformation logic is applied, and data flows through different stages.

A widely adopted pattern to control the flow of data is via the Medallion architecture:

- **Bronze**: Raw, unfiltered data directly from the source.
- **Silver**: Cleaned and structured data, often used for analysis.
- **Gold**: Aggregated and business-ready data, optimized for consumption.

A Data Product, in its inner layout, will use different layers. While the source-aligned might only use a very basic transformation logic (either bronze or silver), a consumer-aligned is using a comprehensive transformation logic, bringing it up to the gold layer.

But one important question remains: do consumer-aligned Data Products always build on top of source-aligned and aggregated

Data Products? If we look at the examples discussed earlier in this chapter, the answer seems to be a clear yes. Building on top of existing layers helps avoid redundant processing and promotes consistency. It also ensures alignment on KPIs, preventing the kind of conflicting metrics we saw in the opening example of this chapter.

To support this layered transformation, data modeling becomes essential. Data models define how data is structured, related, and queried. Depending on the goal, whether it be fast analytics, historical reporting, or compliance, different modeling techniques are applied. These include Star and Snowflake schemas, dimensional modeling, and Data Vault, all of which we will explore in later chapters.

While the technical steps of this phase strongly resemble the Load and Transform components of classic ETL/ELT processes, building a Data Product requires significantly more. A key differentiator is the integration of governance and organizational alignment alongside technical execution. One critical example is Master Data Management (MDM): to ensure consistency and trust, organizations must aim for a golden record. This is a single, authoritative representation of core entities such as customers or products. For instance, the same customer must not appear multiple times across systems under slightly different names. Just have a look at my name – one system might store it as "Mario Meir-Huber", another one as "Meir-Huber, M." and alike.

Achieving this isn't just a matter of implementing deduplication logic. It demands clear data ownership, standardized definitions, and shared accountability across teams. These responsibilities must be embedded into the design and operation of the Data Product and not treated as an afterthought. This is where the GAP triad becomes essential. Technical architecture alone won't deliver high-quality Data Products. Governance ensures clarity and trust in the data. People ensure that standards are understood and upheld. Without this integrated approach, you'll fall back into the same fragmented data landscape you were trying to escape from.

Step 3: Value extraction

The final step for every Data Product is Value Extraction, the stage that completes the DRIVE framework. Unlike traditional ETL/ELT pipelines that often stop after loading or transforming data, Data Products are designed with a very different goal: they must deliver measurable business value. That's why this phase is not an optional add-on, but a core component of the process.

This is where all previous efforts pay off, whether it's building robust ingestion pipelines, integrating data through transformation layers, or ensuring governance and quality. Value Extraction is about putting data into action: enabling decision-making, triggering automated processes, driving operational improvements, enabling AI, or creating new revenue opportunities.

From a business perspective, this phase determines the return on investment. It's the point where data leaves the backend and becomes visible, usable, and impactful to stakeholders—be it in dashboards, APIs, machine learning models, a MCP for AI usage, or operational systems. Without this step, even the most well-architected data pipeline remains just that: a pipeline, not a product.

When we take the metaphor of a car, this is now the product a customer would buy. With this step, we put the paint on the car and make it ready for driving.

Therefore, it needs to be accessible for customers. In Data Products language, this means how to make the Data Product available and what representation it can have. There are numerous ways to achieve that. The most common ones are dashboards or reports. However, it could also be exposed as an API. A representation of a Data Product for AI-driven use-cases is via MCP (model context protocol), or the Data Product could be vectorized to use it for LLMs.

Making a Data Product accessible is one thing, but making it usable is another. This requires several different techniques. First and foremost, clear documentation needs to be provided. Whenever you buy a new product, the first thing you do is to read the documentation. Every Data Product needs to be self-explanatory and contain good documentation. Another thing is training – you can't drive a car without having a driver's license, which requires thorough training. A key strategy here is to upskill people in using the Data Product, either via online training, classroom-styled training, or similar approaches. Training is normally embedded into change management to reduce resistance and get people on board.

Finally, Data Products might also produce money. This can be achieved with data monetization programs. Also, economies around Data Products might develop in the form of Data Spaces or Data Sharing approaches.

As we can see here, it isn't enough to transform data into a technical system; it is more about making it properly usable. This is what Value extraction is all about.

In Data Products terminology, we often speak of "Output Ports" here. These are the artifacts a Data Product produces for its respective users to work with.

CIA – Continuous Improvement and Adaptation

A Data Product is never truly finished. It evolves continuously and must adapt to shifting business needs, technical environments, and user expectations. Markets change, new data sources emerge, and what is cutting-edge today may be obsolete tomorrow.

To remain relevant and valuable, Data Products require ongoing refinement, both in functionality and quality. This includes fixing defects, updating models, incorporating feedback, and optimizing performance. Organizations that fail to invest in this continuous improvement risk falling behind, even if their initial launch was successful.

This principle is called Continuous Improvement and Adaptation. It is not a standalone step; it is a mindset that spans the entire DRIVE process, ensuring that Data Products stay aligned with their purpose and remain a trusted asset throughout their lifecycle.

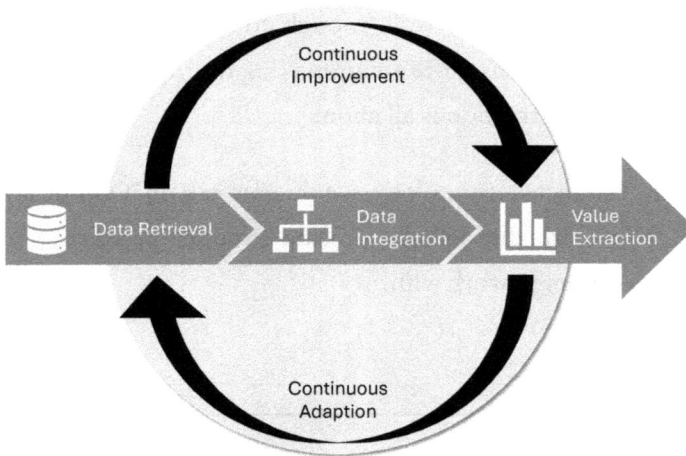

Figure 4: Continuous improvement and adaptation.

Continuous improvement is not an ad-hoc effort. It's a core principle embedded throughout the entire Data Product lifecycle. A central pillar of this is collecting and acting on user feedback on what can be improved. The most effective Data Products are built in close collaboration with their users and are constantly refined to enhance the user experience and business impact.

This is achieved through structured approaches such as A/B testing, usage analytics, or integrated feedback loops. Where feasible, feedback mechanisms can even be embedded directly within the Data Product itself, making it easier to understand what works, what doesn't, and what needs to change.

This phase should not be confused with technical implementation practices such as CI/CD pipelines or DataOps methodologies. These engineering capabilities are foundational enablers that must be embedded throughout the entire DRIVE process. However, they do not represent a separate step in the lifecycle. Instead, they support and automate many of the activities within the core phases, such as deployment, monitoring, or testing. This ensures that Data Products can evolve continuously and reliably. The focus in this step remains on business-driven iteration and lifecycle evolution.

What's next?

Over the past two chapters, we introduced the key frameworks that form the foundation of successful Data Products. The GAP model ensures that each step in the DRIVE process is supported by governance, architecture, and people. The CIA model (Continuous Improvement and Adaptation) guides the ongoing evolution of a Data Product once it's in production. These three frameworks are not meant to be viewed in isolation. They work best when applied together, forming an integrated approach to building and managing high-quality Data Products.

When seen holistically, their interplay looks like Figure 5.

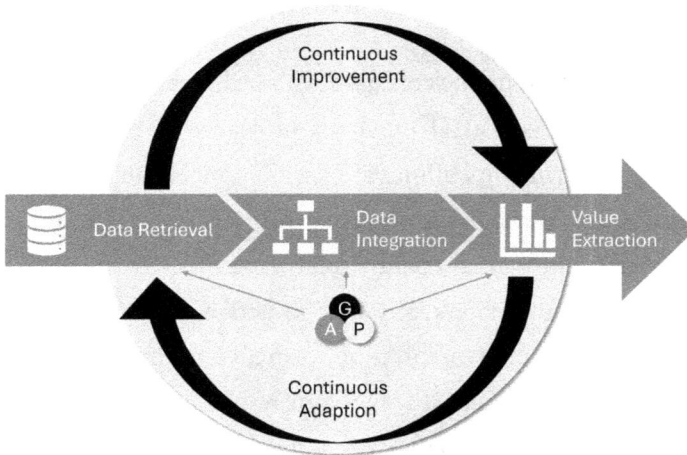

Figure 5: All three frameworks.

Key learnings

- **The DRIVE Framework**: Each step in the lifecycle of a Data Product.
- **Data Retrieval**: The very first step in the lifecycle of a Data Product.
- **Data Integration**: The importance of good data models to power your Data Product.
- **Value Extraction**: How to finally gain value from data.
- **CIA**: How to continuously improve your Data Products.

The Business Dimension

Part II brings in the business aspect of Data Products. Data Products are built to bring impact, and impact is measured in the business. We will learn about measuring this impact and how to build a long-term, strategic roadmap for Data Products. Also, we will look at what it takes to create teams that perform.

FOUR

Practice

Finally, the meeting with our CEO was on the calendar.

A recruiter brought me in to design and launch a new data strategy for a large European organization. Over several weeks, I met with directors, board members, and senior leaders to shape the vision. But there was one major obstacle: funding. Without the CEO's approval, the program would never take off.

In one of those high-stakes boardroom discussions, the CEO leaned back in his chair, looked at me, and said:

"I need to understand this better before I decide. Teach me data science in 30 minutes."

It was both thrilling and terrifying. How do you condense a field that takes years to master into half an hour? Get it right, and the door to multi-million-euro funding could swing wide open. Get it wrong, and the initiative might die before it even begins.

My team and I decided to keep it simple. No buzzwords. No complex models. Just one, relatable example: predicting wine quality using a basic linear regression. We knew the CEO loved red wine, so we turned that into our hook.

The day came. My heart was pounding as I entered his office. He smiled, shook my hand, and asked casually: "So, what are we doing today?"

I walked him through the essentials in ten minutes, then closed my slides and turned my laptop toward him:

"The easiest way to learn is to do. Here's a simple model that scores wine quality based on real data. Let's try it together."

At first, he was hesitant, cautious when I showed him the Jupyter Notebook. But within minutes, curiosity took over. He was running experiments, tweaking inputs, asking sharp questions. Thirty minutes passed. His assistant stepped in to remind him of an important meeting with a VP from a partner company.

"Five more minutes," he said.

Five minutes became thirty. When I finally packed up, he thanked me with a smile that hinted at something more. In the next leadership meeting, he approved the full funding.

I walked out of the CEO's office that day relieved and with full funding secured. But what really stuck with me wasn't just the win. It was the realization that impact isn't created in a Jupyter

Notebook. It is created when the business understands and believes in what you're doing.

That session with the CEO wasn't about teaching the math behind linear regression. It was about making the value of data tangible, relevant, and impossible to ignore. It was a lesson I've carried into every data initiative since: if you can't demonstrate the business impact of your Data Products, they will never make it past the first executive conversation.

And that's exactly what this chapter is about. Data Products are always business-driven, and winning over the business is not optional. It's essential. You will learn how to quantify their impact in ways that resonate with decision-makers. Be it in revenue generation, cost savings, efficiency, or risk reduction. And you will see how to prioritize and roadmap Data Products so they align with your organization's strategic goals.

The most powerful Data Products aren't the ones with the most sophisticated architecture.
They're the ones the business can't afford to live without.

Calculating the value of a data product

A Data Product must always deliver tangible value to someone, without exception. As we established in Chapter 1, value is its very reason for existence. In this chapter, we take a closer look at what that means in practice.

The most obvious and measurable form of value is financial impact. This can take many forms: generating new revenue, reducing operational costs, or improving efficiency. We will break down the different ways to quantify this impact and show how to link it directly to business outcomes.

But value isn't always about the bottom line. Data Products can also deliver significant non-financial benefits, such as reducing regulatory or operational risk, unlocking new strategic capabilities, enabling faster decision-making, and driving innovation. These benefits may be harder to measure, but they can be equally critical in driving adoption and securing stakeholder buy-in.

Measuring the financial impact

At first glance, measuring the financial impact of a Data Product seems straightforward. It's just numbers. Surely, they're easy to calculate, right? In reality, it's one of the most challenging tasks you'll face. The difficulty rarely comes from complex formulas or advanced mathematics. More often, the real barrier is human: people's reluctance to commit to concrete savings, revenue projections, or efficiency gains, because doing so creates accountability and pressure.

But let's put the organizational challenges aside and focus on the fundamentals: understanding the different types of financial impact a Data Product can have and how to calculate them in a practical and credible way.

The financial impact of a Data Product can typically be measured across four dimensions:

- Cost reductions through higher productivity and resource optimization
- Increased revenues from cross-selling and upselling
- New revenues from data monetization or entirely new products
- Efficiency gains from faster processes and improved employee enablement.

While each of these stems from specific use cases, their calculation methodologies are often similar. The starting point is always understanding the full cost of a Data Product. Building one is never free, yet its benefits must clearly outweigh its costs. When a Data Product is implemented the right way (as outlined in previous chapters), costs can be minimized. A significant reduction can be achieved through shared platforms and reusable data models, avoiding the need to reinvent the wheel for every Data Product.

The total cost of a Data Product is made up of several distinct components. Understanding these cost blocks is essential for budgeting, prioritization, and ensuring the product delivers a positive return. Let's break down the key cost categories involved in developing and maintaining a Data Product.

Total cost of ownership for Data Products

The main costs for a new Data Product are often only measured in development costs. While they normally account for a large share of direct costs, they are often very high at the beginning and then decrease as a Data Product matures. Even if your teams are fully internal ones, it is essential to calculate an internal cost factor for this development.

We also need to consider the technology and infrastructure costs. Depending on how you run your Data Products, you either need new software licenses and potentially also hardware, or your cloud costs will rise. Especially the latter one is easier to calculate, as you can apply FinOps by tagging each Data Product's cost. Developing high-quality Data Products can reduce cost factors on a large scale.

Not the highest costs, but still relevant costs are the costs of integration. If you provide your Data Products via APIs or dashboards, costs might be zero or close to it, but in many cases, your Data Products need to be integrated into other products. If you develop churn models, you might want to have the results in your POS or CRM Systems. This normally creates costs with other teams that implement these solutions. If you don't budget for this in your Data Product, you might end up in endless discussions about how to integrate it and get low priority with these teams.

A Data Product is never finished, so it is essential to continuously develop it. Running your Data Product thus creates additional costs. These are either the costs for the team that continuously develops new features or simply the costs of someone operating it. Costs here are typically not very high, but still are something you need to consider.

Data Products always come with a strong regulatory and legal component. Different regions of the world have various legal systems. When you build your Data Product at a global scale, you need to budget for legal advice and for implementing features in accordance with local laws. This can be tricky, since tech people are typically very unfamiliar with legal terminology.

Last but not least, it is important to train and upskill people to work with your Data Products. This could be for internal training and enablement, or for external use if you monetize your Data Products.

The following tables summarize the cost factors split into one-time expenses and continuous expenses:

One-Time Costs

Cost Type	Description
Development Costs	Might be high if it requires longer setup cycles, or could also be embedded in ongoing development
Integration Costs	Normally happens once
Regulatory advice	Normally happens once

Continuous Costs

Cost Type	Description
Development Costs	Might be decreasing over time but could also be continuous
Technology and Infrastructure Costs	Software, hardware, or cloud costs
Operational Costs	Costs of running (without cloud costs)
Training	Costs for continuous training

Depending on the project, one-time costs can represent a substantial investment. This is particularly true when a Data Product must be developed from scratch, without leveraging an existing platform or data models. These costs often include initial architecture design, tooling setup, and foundational engineering work. In programs with multiple Data Products under development, these costs can be amortized across them, reducing the burden on individual products and improving overall ROI.

Let's say a bank plans to build a completely new Data Product, a reporting platform for customer service, from scratch. Their existing data warehouse has reached capacity, and the data it contains is no longer reliable. The business has committed to a Data Product approach and agreed to develop it in short, Agile cycles, avoiding large up-front investments.

A significant cost driver is the rollout across multiple global regions (the US, Latin America, Europe, and Asia), which will require extensive legal support to ensure compliance with local regulations, including GDPR and banking privacy laws. Because the platform will run entirely in the cloud, most costs will be operational rather than capital expenditures, with no need for major software license purchases. However, operational costs are expected to increase gradually over the next four years, making long-term cost management and FinOps practices critical.

The costs for Capex are:

Initial setup costs	$100,000
Legal advice	$50,000
Integration costs	$10,000

The costs for Opex are:

	Year 1	Year 2	Year 3	Year 4
Development costs	$1,200,000	$1,000,000	$800,000	$600,000
Cloud Costs	$25,000	$50,000	$150,000	$250,000
Operations cost	$50,000	$50,000	$50,000	$50,000
Training and Upskilling	$20000	$10,000	$5,000	$0

In this example, the one-time costs amount to $160,000. The yearly operating costs vary over time: development costs decrease as the Data Product matures, while cloud costs increase as more customer service staff actively use the platform. Over a four-year period, the total operating costs amount to roughly $4.3 million.

Adding the one-time costs results in a total cost of ownership (TCO) of approximately $4.46 million. This calculation excludes potential interest or discount rate effects, which may be relevant in certain financial models but are not considered here.

Understanding this cost profile is essential before assessing the platform's return on investment. With this in mind, let's move to the financial benefits and the formulas used to quantify the value of Data Products.

Financial benefits

Data Products exist to create measurable business value, and financial benefits are often the most compelling driver for their adoption. These benefits typically fall into four main clusters:

- **Cost reduction**: Lowering operational costs is a priority for every executive. Data Products can automate repetitive work, streamline workflows, and improve resource planning. They can also replace outdated systems and legacy data assets, which are often expensive to maintain. Modern Data Products are typically more cost-efficient because they avoid the complexity of legacy stacks.

- **Revenue growth**: By enabling targeted cross-selling and upselling, or enhancing the overall customer experience, Data Products directly contribute to top-line growth. Decisions on which customers to target, what products to offer, and when to engage are increasingly data-driven.

- **New revenue streams**: Some Data Products can be offered externally, turning data into a marketable asset.

Examples range from Google Analytics to sector-specific analytics services. Monetizing data is not without risk, but when executed well, it can open entirely new business lines.

- **Efficiency gains**: Faster processes free up employee time, improve customer satisfaction, and accelerate product delivery.

Often, a single Data Product delivers benefits across multiple clusters. For the bank, replacing multiple regional systems reduces infrastructure and operational costs, decommissions costly data warehouses, and eliminates redundant roles. At the same time, it enables cross-selling and upselling opportunities that directly boost revenue.

How to calculate the financial aspects

A major obstacle in calculating the financial benefit of a Data Product is securing business unit commitment to the projected results. Without alignment on the numbers, ROI calculations risk becoming political rather than factual. One proven way to address this is the Delphi Method.

This approach gathers input from multiple subject-matter experts across the business on the expected financial impact of a Data Product. In the first round of interviews, estimates often vary widely. The consolidated, anonymized results are then shared back with the experts, who participate in a second round of estimation. This process typically narrows the range of answers and moves the group toward a shared, evidence-based projection. Repeat the rounds of estimation multiple times until the group reaches a common estimation. The Delphi Method is often used for forecasting financial results and is a proven method for this.

Let's revisit the bank example introduced earlier in this chapter. After applying the Delphi Method with a selected group of business and technical experts, we consolidated their estimates for the Data Product's financial benefits:

Type	Year 1	Year 2	Year 4	Year 5
Cost Reduction—HW	$0	$0	$500,000	$0
Cost Reduction—SW	$0	$0	$1,500,000	$0

New Revenues from upselling	$10,000	$250,000	$600,000	$1,400,000
Revenues from returning customers	$5,000	$150,000	$400,000	$1,000,000

Workforce improvement	$0	$0	$200,000	$500,000

As shown in the example above, the financial benefits of the Data Product come from multiple sources and not only from generating new revenue. A significant, but often overlooked, share arises from cost reductions, as the bank doesn't need to renew the legacy reporting database or the associated hardware.

Major gains are achieved through improved upselling opportunities, driven by more accurate and timely customer insights. The enhanced customer experience also increases purchase frequency and retention, amplifying lifetime value. While further revenue could be calculated from an improved Net Promoter Score (NPS), the current analysis focuses on the most direct impacts.

Finally, workforce efficiency improves as the new Data Product replaces several fragmented reporting solutions across regions, reducing duplicate roles and labor costs.

Having these numbers is a significant milestone. The next step is to translate them into concrete metrics. The first, and often the most straightforward, is Return on Investment (ROI), a key measure for evaluating the financial viability of any Data Product. The formula is:

(Revenues – Investment costs) / Investment costs

The result of applying this formula is the ROI, expressed as a percentage. In our bank example, this calculation results in:

($6,515,000 – $4,470,000) / $4,470,000

This results in an ROI of 51% over the first four years. Beyond that period, the ROI is likely to rise further as development costs decrease, and the Data Product continues to generate higher returns from new revenue streams.

While ROI shows whether the revenue outweighs the investment, another critical metric is the break-even analysis. This method answers a question every CFO will ask: When will the Data Product start generating net positive returns? ROI tells us how much value we get; break-even tells us when that value begins. The formula for break-even is:

Σ(Revenues per Year) – (Fixed cost + Σ(Variable Costs per Year)) >= 0

This calculation is repeated year by year until the cumulative net result turns positive. That is the point at which the Data Product has recovered its costs and starts generating net revenue. For our bank Data Product, this would be:

Year 1: -$1,280,000
Year 2: -$1,990,000
Year 3: $205,000

This means the Data Product will reach its break-even point in the third year. When combined with the ROI figure, this gives a powerful narrative for executives. We can clearly state in leadership meetings that the solution not only pays for itself within three years but will continue to generate increasing returns thereafter. We can craft this message:

The new Data Product will break even within three years and generate a 51% return on investment over the first four years, with profitability accelerating beyond that point.

This is a powerful message that can secure executive approval for the investment case. But beyond winning funding, it provides a clear, measurable foundation for tracking success over time. Financial impact, expressed in ROI and break-even terms, turns the concept of a Data Product from a technical initiative into a tangible business asset. The ability to articulate this value in simple, credible numbers is what will keep stakeholders aligned, budgets secured, and priorities intact. With this clarity, the conversation shifts from "Why should we invest?" to "How fast can we scale?" This is the discussion we need for Data Products.

Non-financial impact

Not all benefits of Data Products can be expressed in financial terms. While I believe most outcomes can be linked to a measurable business impact, some factors resist direct monetary quantification. Before diving into the truly non-financial benefits, it's worth clarifying a few areas that are often misunderstood and prematurely labeled as "impossible" to measure:

- **Improved decision-making**: This sits at the borderline between financial and non-financial benefits. Faster, better-informed decisions can protect market share and secure planned growth. Delays, on the other hand, can result in competitive losses, underscoring the importance of this capability for long-term success.

- **Improved knowledge sharing**: Often seen as a "secondary benefit" of data governance, improved accessibility of Data Products has a direct operational impact. It increases organizational efficiency, frees up workforce capacity, and optimizes technology usage.

Well-governed data use also prevents uncontrolled cloud cost growth by encouraging sustainable consumption.

- **Foundation for AI**: AI relies on quality data as its core fuel. Investing in the data layer is not a separate initiative but a prerequisite for AI-driven value creation. A mature Data Product doesn't stop at data exposure, it integrates seamlessly with the AI stack. As a result, AI-generated revenues and benefits should also be attributed to the underlying Data Product.

Now, let's focus on the true non-financial benefits of Data Products. They fall into two main themes: strategic relevance, which strengthens competitive positioning, and legal necessity, which ensures compliance and reduces regulatory risk.

A Data Product may have strategic relevance simply because a competitor excels at it. While this can overlap with lost-revenue considerations, some Data Products have no direct numerical impact, yet are still necessary to deliver. In my experience, only a small number truly fall into this category. They are most often in highly regulated industries or in corporate cultures where their delivery is expected.

The second driver is legal necessity. Different industries and regions operate under legal frameworks that mandate the creation of specific Data Products. For example, in the telecom sector, operators must provide location data to law enforcement for crime prevention—often in real time. The cost of delivering such

Data Products rarely supports a positive business case. In the European banking sector, institutions are required to produce extensive financial stability reports, such as those under IFRS and European Central Bank regulations. These projects involve consolidating large volumes of data and are undertaken solely to meet regulatory obligations, not to generate direct financial returns.

Aligning business goals and technical roadmap

While calculating the financial impact is easy for a single Data Product, we often encounter Data Products in complex corporate environments. Different units within an organization battle for budget and they want to build their own Data Products. While this is a good approach since decentralization is a key aspect of Data Products, it isn't easy because budgets in large organizations are always limited. This makes a joint roadmap essential for aligning on enterprise-wide priorities.

Building such a roadmap is challenging, even with the financial insights from the previous section. Relying solely on business and financial metrics—an approach common in the past—has led to significant issues: data governance was overlooked, silo consolidation was never addressed, and funding often went to the loudest revenue promises rather than the most feasible projects. The result was failed initiatives, with IT teams seen as incapable and business units viewed as unrealistic in their expectations.

To avoid repeating these mistakes, both business and IT perspectives must be unified in the roadmap process. In this sub-chapter, we will explore a matrix designed to bring these worlds together and create a balanced, executable plan.

We'll start with an illustration of the matrix, then break down its different axes. Here's the full picture:

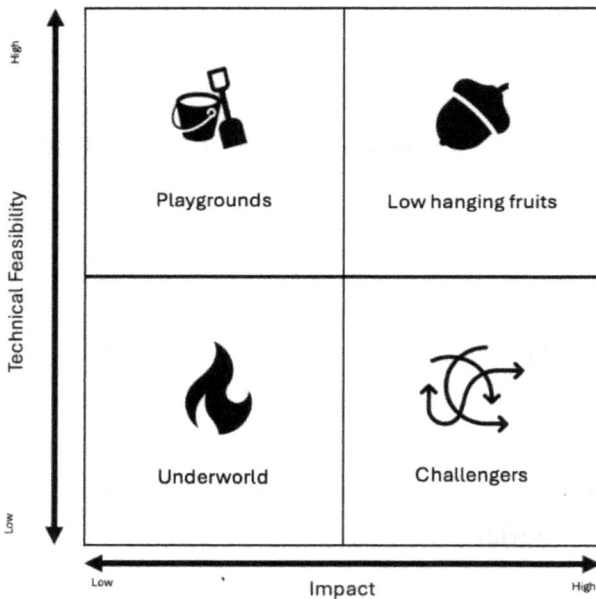

Figure 6: Impact and technical feasibility.

The matrix in Figure 6 contains two major dimensions: impact and technical feasibility. We will begin with impact. In this context, impact refers to the financial or strategic value, as discussed earlier. Measuring the financial impact is straightforward, but mapping strategic impact onto the matrix is more challenging.

To make both comparable, we normalize financial figures into a common 0–10 scale. The impact axis, therefore, ranges from 0 (low) to ten (high). Financial returns can be mapped directly, while strategically critical Data Products can be assigned high scores even with negative ROI.

Let's use an example to illustrate this:

- Data Product A – ROI 110% → Score 8
- Data Product B – ROI 25% → Score 0
- Data Product C – ROI 90% → Score 6
- Data Product D – ROI 150% → Score 10
- Data Product E – ROI –15% but regulatory necessity → Score 10

This approach allows both financial and strategic priorities to be plotted on the same axis, making it possible to compare Data Products objectively in the matrix.

The second dimension is technical feasibility. While this will be examined in detail shortly, we will make some initial assumptions here to proceed with the matrix. Scores range from 0 (not feasible to execute) to ten (easy to execute).

The principle is straightforward: high technical feasibility means the organization can build the Data Product efficiently; low feasibility indicates a high risk of failure or prohibitively high implementation costs.

Example scores:

- Data Product A – Score 8
- Data Product B – Score 10
- Data Product C – Score 9
- Data Product D – Score 3
- Data Product E – Score 6

With both dimensions now scored, we can plot the Data Products onto the matrix for visual comparison.

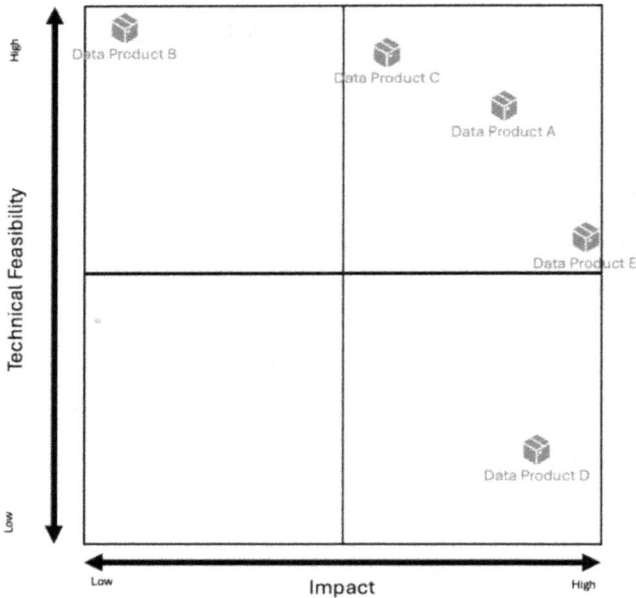

Figure 7: Matrix example.

What remains is a description of the four quadrants in the matrix. While their meaning may seem obvious, we will outline them briefly for completeness:

- **Low-hanging fruits**: High-impact Data Products that are technically easy to deliver. These should be top priorities for every organization.

- **Challengers**: High-impact Data Products that are difficult to implement. Before starting, remove technical barriers or increase the organization's technical maturity.

- **Playgrounds**: Low-impact Data Products that require little effort to deliver. They can be useful for onboarding new developers or as exploratory projects to refine their potential value.

- **Underground**: Low-impact and difficult to deliver. These offer little value and carry high risk; they should generally be avoided.

With this framework in place, organizations should focus on executing projects in the first quadrant—the Low Hanging Fruits—while developing a roadmap to improve technical feasibility for the challengers.

In most companies I have consulted, the majority of data projects fell into the Challengers quadrant. (I am explicitly talking about data projects here, as most companies didn't build real Data Products as defined in the previous chapters.) Low technical maturity made these projects difficult to execute. The reasons varied, but a common pattern emerged: organizations rarely aligned business impact with technical feasibility, leaving them without an overarching implementation strategy. Many also failed to address technical blockers or invest in raising platform maturity.

This framework changes that. By plotting all projects on the matrix, it becomes easy to quantify the potential unlocked by improving technical capabilities. For example, summing the impact scores of all projects in the challengers quadrant reveals the total business value at stake.

The logic is simple:
remove complexity and increase feasibility,
and you release the full impact of these Data Products.

In practice, the number of Data Products is often far higher than in our example. I have worked with organizations managing 50-60 such initiatives, yet they are only able to deliver around 15 per year. That meant some projects were delayed by up to four years. This was frustrating for those waiting at the end of the roadmap. Improving technical capabilities shortens delivery cycles, making prioritization easier and enabling more projects to be completed sooner.

Another recurring challenge is the tendency to prioritize high-impact projects without considering technical feasibility. Without this measure, organizations frequently commit to complex initiatives with long runtimes, escalating costs, and missed deadlines.

The strength of this framework is that it unites technical excellence and business value in a single view. It enables leaders to choose initiatives that deliver meaningful impact and can be executed effectively. In the next section, we will examine technical feasibility in detail.

Measuring technical feasibility

How do we measure technical feasibility for Data Products? We don't need to reinvent the wheel here: the GAP Framework we already know from Chapter two provides exactly the right lens. Each of its three dimensions can help us assess feasibility in a structured way.

A key point is to distinguish between fixed parameters and variable parameters. Fixed parameters apply to every Data Product, regardless of use case. Variable parameters, on the other hand, differ across Data Products and must be assessed individually.

It's also important to note the perspective here. In Chapter 2, we described the desired characteristics of a Data Product. In this section, however, we are focusing on the step before building one. That means we won't reuse the product aspects directly; instead, we'll apply GAP to help organizations decide whether a Data Product can realistically be delivered.

Governance

Fixed parameters:

- **Metadata and catalog**: A well-managed metadata repository (including glossary and lineage) clarifies what data the organization owns and how it's defined. Proper stewardship benefits all Data Products.

- **Access and discoverability**: Self-service access with clear approval workflows and entitlements reduces lead time to data and speeds up delivery.

- **Baseline compliance**: Organization-wide policies for classification, retention, and audit logging ensure every Data Product meets the minimum legal and security requirements.

- **Standards and contracts**: Required naming conventions, KPI definitions, and data contracts set a consistent "floor" for quality and interoperability.

Variable parameters:

- **Regulatory scope**: Feasibility varies by jurisdiction, data sensitivity (e.g., PII), and required assessments. Some Data Products are straightforward, while others are legally complex.

- **Data quality readiness**: Quality can differ by source or business unit. If the producing team enforces strong quality controls, the Data Product is easier to deliver, while weak upstream quality increases risk and effort.

- **Sharing posture**: Internal-only, partner sharing, or external monetization each changes legal terms, approvals, and timelines.

Architecture

Fixed parameters:

- **Shared platform availability**: Is there a common data platform with shared data models and services, or does each Data Product require its own build-out? A shared platform reduces lead time and risk.

Variable parameters:

- **Data volume**: Higher volumes raise processing cost and complexity. This might require additional compute, storage, or partitioning strategies. Also, cloud usage will be higher.

- **Scalability and freshness**: Real-time or near-real-time needs versus batch processing (daily, hourly) change architecture choices and cost profiles. Also, note whether source systems can emit real-time events even when consumers need them.

- **Reuse of other Data Products**: Availability of upstream, composable Data Products (with stable interfaces and contracts) reduces effort, whereas absence increases integration work. This reflects the composability of Data Products and plays favorably if done well.

- **Source availability and integration depth**: Are the required sources already connected to the shared platform? New systems, custom connectors, or legacy interfaces increase scope and risk.

People

Fixed parameters:

- **Data ownership**: A clear, enterprise-wide data ownership model ensures that the data needed to build Data Products is actively managed and stewarded. Because this is typically defined at the company level, it is either present for all Data Products or missing entirely, making it a largely fixed feasibility factor.

- **Change management capability**: Mature change management practices help business units adopt new Data Products and adjust processes, roles, and behaviors accordingly. When this capability exists and is embedded, every Data Product benefits from faster adoption and fewer roll-out risks.

Variable parameters:

- **Team expertise and capacity**: Feasibility depends on whether the delivery team has the skills and bandwidth required for the specific product—be that API design, streaming pipelines, ML/LLM integration, or advanced analytics. If gaps exist, you will need to plan training, hiring, or partner support to keep timelines realistic.

- **Stakeholder buy-in and sponsorship**: Success hinges on whether target users and their leaders believe in the product and are willing to change how they work. Top-down mandates without grassroots support often trigger resistance; early engagement and visible sponsorship mitigate this risk and improve feasibility.

- **Partner and vendor dependency**: When implementation partners operate systems or when key data resides in vendor platforms, contracting, access, and delivery schedules can materially affect feasibility. The ease of bringing partners on board should be assessed explicitly.

Weighting and scoring each aspect

Now that we understand the key feasibility factors, the next step is to assign weights to the three dimensions. All three matter, but in many organizations, architecture drives the bulk of delivery risk and cost, so it receives a slightly higher weight than governance, followed by people.

A pragmatic starting point is:

- Governance: 32.5%
- Architecture: 37.5%
- People: 30.0%

Treat these figures as a baseline rather than a doctrine. Adjust them to your context. For example, highly regulated environments may increase the governance weight, while greenfield teams with significant skill gaps may increase the people weight. For the worked example in this chapter, we will use the matrix above.

In our bank's case, baseline compliance and change management are in good shape, but governance is uneven: metadata and standards are weak, and access and discoverability are a clear gap. Architecturally, the landscape is fragmented with no shared platform, which limits reuse and raises delivery risk. The organization can absorb change, but it still lacks the foundations such as clear data ownership, a usable catalog, and a common platform to scale Data Products reliably.

We will begin by scoring the fixed parameters at the organizational level, because these apply across all Data Products and can be reused. For the bank introduced earlier, this looks as follows:

Governance:

- Metadata and catalog: Not in place; some ad-hoc documentation on an internal site. Score: 3

- Access and discoverability: Poorly implemented across the organization; hard to find and request data. Score: 2

- Baseline compliance: Large-enterprise legal requirements are enforced; controls exist. Score: 8

- Standards and contracts: Naming/KPI standards and data contracts are largely missing or inconsistently applied. Score: 3

Architecture:

- Shared platform availability: Multiple platforms by country/business unit; limited reuse and fragmentation. Score: 2

People:

- Data ownership: Largely absent; unclear stewards for key domains. Score: 2

- Change-management capability: HR has mature change management practices we can leverage. Score: 8

The tricky part now is with the variable parameters, as we need to score every Data Product. We will do this for two Data Products. The first Data Product is the customer service reporting dashboard from earlier in the chapter. The other one is a risk-scoring API.

Let's begin with the reporting dashboard for customer service, which we already introduced. This Data Product handles highly sensitive information, as it displays customer-related data. While data quality has historically been poor, the goal of this new implementation is to rebuild integrations from the ground up to ensure consistency and accuracy.

One of the main challenges is the requirement for near real-time data ingestion, with a maximum delay of 15 minutes—a demand strongly emphasized by engaged stakeholders. Fortunately, the overall data volume is manageable, especially due to the frequent refresh intervals, which keep each data load relatively small. The Data Product team has collaborated closely with the business unit and has a clear understanding of its expectations. The planned tools are already in use within the organization, and external dependencies are minimal.

The second Data Product is an API requested by the purchasing department. The company works with numerous global suppliers and frequently encounters issues related to supplier credit risk, especially in underdeveloped regions. These risks have led to significant financial losses. In response, the purchasing team proposed a Data Product that delivers real-time credit scoring of suppliers by integrating and analyzing multiple data sources.

This solution combines structured data on financial health and transaction history with unstructured data from online sources. A large language model (LLM) processes public web content to detect potential risks, while a machine learning model consolidates these findings into a comprehensive risk score. Although the algorithm is compute-intensive, it only needs to run 10–30 times per day, based on queries from the purchasing department.

However, several challenges exist. There is no history of collaboration with the department, and initial feedback suggests a lack of internal support. The required data must be procured from external vendors, and the implementation involves advanced technologies unfamiliar to the current data team. These factors introduce uncertainty around team readiness and partner dependency.

We now take these two Data Products and score them against the parameters in the table below. The scoring comes from the above description. We create categories for GAP and divide them into fixed and variable parameters:

Parameter	Data Product 1: Customer Service Dashboard	Data Product 2: Supplier Risk Scoring API
Governance		
Fixed Parameters		
Metadata and catalog	3	3
Access and discoverability	2	2
Baseline compliance	8	8
Standards and contracts	3	3
Variable Parameters		
Regulatory scope	4	8
Data quality readiness	3	2
Sharing posture	10	8
Architecture		
Fixed Parameters		
Shared platform availability	2	2
Variable Parameters		
Data volume	7	8
Scalability and freshness	4	6
Reuse of other Data Products	2	2
Source availability and integration depth	4	2
People		
Fixed Parameters		
Data ownership	2	2
Change management capability	8	8
Variable Parameters		
Team expertise and capacity	9	3
Stakeholder buy-in and sponsorship	10	2
Partner and vendor dependency	9	2

Based on the weighted scores, the first Data Product (the Customer Service Dashboard) achieves a technical feasibility score of 5.24, while the second (the Supplier Risk API) scores 4.10. Assuming both have a strong business impact (rated at eight and seven respectively), this positions the Customer Service Dashboard at the lower end of the "Low-Hanging Fruits" quadrant, while the Supplier Risk API falls into the "Challengers" quadrant.

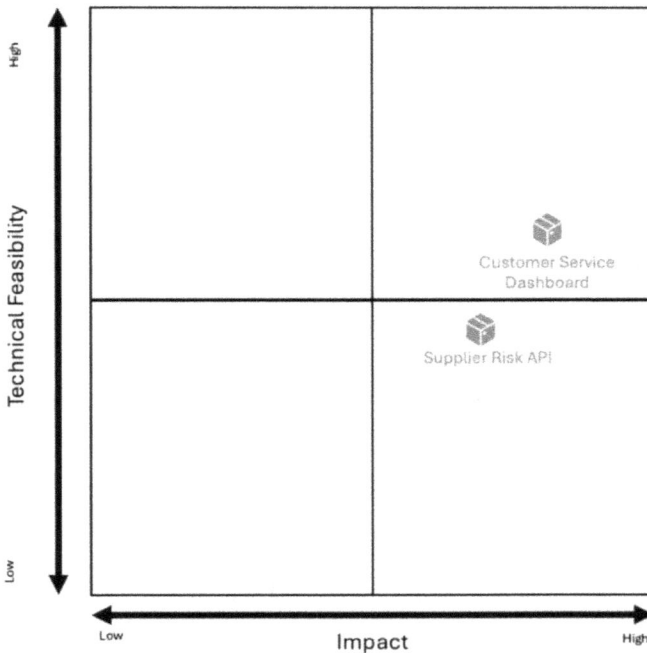

Figure 8: Supplier Risk and Customer Service.

However, neither Data Product performs particularly well overall, primarily due to weaknesses in the fixed parameters, especially around data governance. This highlights a broader organizational issue to address. Shortly, we will explore how to systematically improve these foundations to boost feasibility scores across all future Data Products.

While this approach is well-suited for building a comprehensive enterprise Data Product roadmap, it also proves valuable when working on a single, complex Data Product. In that case, instead of comparing multiple products, you can break the Data Product down into its key features or components and evaluate them individually. This demonstrates the flexibility of the framework, allowing you to adapt it to your specific context, whether you're managing a portfolio or refining a single initiative.

Prioritizing for roadmap execution

With the framework introduced in this chapter, it becomes straightforward to build an actionable Data Product roadmap. We can clearly identify which initiatives to prioritize—namely, those in the "Low Hanging Fruits" quadrant. But beyond prioritization by impact, the framework also helps us understand which technical and organizational obstacles may hinder execution.

In our case, several fixed parameters stand out as barriers to feasibility: the lack of a shared data platform, limited discoverability due to missing metadata catalogs, and the absence of clearly defined data ownership. If we focus our investment on improving these three foundational elements, we can shift multiple Data Products from the "Challengers" quadrant into "Low Hanging Fruits." For example, if we raise their respective scores to eight (indicating significant improvement), the feasibility scores of the Customer Service Dashboard and Supplier Risk API increase to 6.20 and 5.06, respectively.

Now imagine applying this uplift across your entire Data Product portfolio. If ten high-value Data Products shift into an executable state, each with an estimated value of $1.5 million, you could unlock $15 million in business benefit. That makes it significantly easier to justify a $2 million investment in platform, cataloging, and ownership initiatives. The value unlocked far exceeds the cost.

This framework does more than just help you decide which Data Product to prioritize. It guides you toward the concrete actions needed to make them successful. By systematically identifying barriers and improvement levers, it enables organizations to move from isolated, siloed efforts to a coordinated and scalable Data Product strategy. It ensures that foundational investments, such as shared platforms, clear ownership, and improved metadata, are aligned with business outcomes. In doing so, it bridges the gap between long-term architectural excellence and immediate business value.

It's not a choice between fixing the basics or delivering results. This framework allows you to do both.

It's also important to recognize that technology evolves rapidly. What is considered state-of-the-art today may be outdated in just a few years. For example, not long ago, Hadoop was widely adopted and seen as the industry standard. Yet today, many organizations are actively replacing their Hadoop stacks, now viewed as legacy infrastructure. This highlights the need to regularly revisit your prioritization framework to ensure that your Data Product strategy remains aligned with current technological standards and organizational needs.

Key learnings

- **Measuring impact**: A Data Product can have two key impact factors: a financial one and a strategic one.

- **Impact and feasibility**: If a Data Product has a high (financial) impact, it doesn't necessarily mean that it is the right thing to implement, especially when the organization isn't ready for it.

- **Measuring feasibility**: feasibility is derived from the GAP thinking we learned about earlier.

- **Building a roadmap**: Addressing the Data Products for early execution while improving capabilities in the organization.

FIVE

Scalability

Monday, 11 a.m.

I entered the auditorium right on time. It was a full department meeting, one I had been preparing for months. The stakes were high, and it was clear to everyone that something important was about to happen. The tension in the room was palpable. Only a few of my direct managers knew what was coming: a major restructuring of how we work with data.

Six months earlier, I had just started in my new role. Eager to understand the current setup, I asked one of my team leads to show me the existing process for bringing new use cases into production. What he showed me was a slide packed with boxes, arrows, and lines. It was so complex it barely fit the screen. I looked at the chart, looked at him, and said:

"Please close it. I don't want to see this again. We're going to change the process."

What followed was six months of intense effort. Moving from waterfall to agile isn't new, but in data teams, it's rarely straightforward. Together with HR, we planned a new organizational setup designed to deliver faster, better, and more aligned to business needs. When I finally stood in front of the team to explain the changes, I was nervous. How would the team react? Would we lose key talent?

But the response surprised me. After the meeting, several colleagues came forward to express their support. In the end, only two people left the company. Both had performance issues. A year later, the entire organization had adopted the model we pioneered in our unit.

In this chapter, we'll take a closer look at how to design organizational structures that enable Data Product success. We'll explore the key roles needed, how to build teams around business delivery and technical excellence, and what management practices help drive execution. Whether you're building a small Data Product unit or scaling to the enterprise level, this chapter is about turning strategy into structure.

Decentral? Central? Hybrid!

Designing Data Product teams is one of the most debated topics in modern data organizations. Some argue for a centralized IT model, where specialized expertise is pooled and governed centrally. Others, particularly within business units, push for decentralization, claiming that proximity to the business is critical for delivering real value. Frameworks like Data Mesh further reinforce this argument by emphasizing domain ownership and distributed responsibilities.

But decentralization also has trade-offs. It can make it difficult to staff rare roles, such as ML engineers or data architects, in every unit. Larger enterprises often lean toward hybrid models, where some roles are embedded in the business while others remain centralized for scale and consistency.

In this section, we'll dive into the strengths and weaknesses of both centralized and decentralized team models. I've worked with organizations that followed either approach. In most cases, the results fell short of expectations. The real challenge isn't in choosing one model over the other, but in understanding the conditions and design principles that make them successful. Like in previous chapters, this model applies to large enterprises. If you are a startup that builds exactly one Data Product, the question of decentral versus central doesn't really come up.

Decentral setup

Data is inherently decentralized. There's no way around it. Business units generate and use data in different ways, and it's only logical to assume that data teams should sit close to where the data lives. A decentralized setup reflects this reality, and in many cases, it brings speed and proximity to business needs. But it's not without challenges.

Let's begin with the downsides. One of the most common pitfalls of decentralized data teams is the lack of alignment. Without a central authority or shared standards, it becomes difficult to enforce consistency in data modeling, access tools, or integration approaches (see Chapters 6, 7, and 8). This often leads to incompatible data models, fragmented tools, and regulatory blind spots, especially around sensitive data such as PII. The absence of shared guardrails creates a governance drift that is hard to control at scale.

Moreover, decentralization can hinder the true potential of Data Products. Composability becomes difficult when teams follow their own interpretations of how data should be structured and exposed. In the worst cases, the same business metric is calculated differently in separate units, undermining trust in the data and sparking executive-level debates. You don't want data alignment discussions to happen in the boardroom.

From a resourcing perspective, decentralization can also be inefficient. Scarce roles such as data engineers, architects, or AI engineers might sit idle in some units while overloaded in others. Without coordinated planning, duplicated efforts and redundant infrastructure costs are almost inevitable.

However, there are strong arguments for decentralization. Since data originates in business domains, those domains are best suited to manage it. Decentralized teams understand their own processes and goals deeply, and that makes them better equipped to define and deliver relevant Data Products. Centralized teams, especially those with a purely technical mandate, often lack this contextual understanding.

Speed is another important benefit. Decentralized teams can move faster because they avoid cross-departmental prioritization processes and lengthy approval cycles. This enables them to respond more quickly to evolving business needs and deliver tangible results in shorter timeframes.

Central setup

A centralized setup stands in stark contrast to a decentralized approach. Historically, most data initiatives followed a centralized model. However, its shortcomings, particularly around responsiveness, have often been cited as reasons to shift toward decentralization.

One of the central model's biggest weaknesses is speed and time-to-market. Central teams tend to be large, and decision-making can be slow. Prioritization is often complex due to limited budgets, meaning only a small fraction of use cases can be executed. This leads to frustration within business units and, in many cases, results in the creation of local silos while waiting for central support. Central teams can quickly become implementation bottlenecks.

Another challenge lies in the limited business context of central teams, especially when they sit within IT departments. This often results in extended coordination loops to gather domain knowledge and align on requirements. Centralized teams may struggle to fully understand business needs, leading to inefficient or misaligned solutions.

Despite these challenges, the centralized model offers significant benefits. It ensures consistency in platform usage and data models, which simplifies technical data governance. Silos are less likely to emerge, and the overall data architecture remains more coherent. Platform maintenance is typically easier, and costs are more predictable and controllable. Furthermore, quality checks and the financial impact of poor data quality can be monitored and managed more effectively.

Comparing both

Unfortunately, there is no definitive winner when comparing centralized and decentralized approaches. Both models offer advantages and trade-offs, and neither provides a one-size-fits-all solution.

The following table summarizes the key differences between centralized and decentralized models, with a particular focus on their impact on Data Products. It begins with a comparison of business and technical dimensions, then extends to additional considerations unique to each setup (decentral versus central) as discussed earlier in this section. Note that this is a neutral stance; if the organization is extremely decentralized, certain aspects in the table below might shift in favor or vice versa for a centralized organization.

	Decentral	Central
Business Dimension		
Clear Purpose and consumer relevance	★★★	★☆☆
Usability and readiness	★☆☆	★★☆
Reliability and transparency	★★☆	★★★
Understandable and self-describing	★★☆	★☆☆
Approved and up to date	★★★	★☆☆
Technical Dimension		
Composable and interoperable	★☆☆	★★★
Trustworthy, secure, and reliable	★★☆	★★★
Discoverable and addressable	★☆☆	★★★
Shared platform and models	★☆☆	★★★
Robust	★☆☆	★★★
Data quality and integrity management	★☆☆	★★☆
Monitoring and observability	★☆☆	★★★
Setup-specific Dimensions		
Common data models	★☆☆	★★★
Alignment effort	★☆☆	★★★
Cost efficiency	★☆☆	★★★
Governance drift	★☆☆	★★★
Data Ownership	★★★	★☆☆

While the setup-specific differences were already discussed in detail, it is worth briefly revisiting how the business and technical dimensions of Data Products are influenced by the chosen organizational model.

A clear purpose is rooted in a deep understanding of the business domain, something business units are naturally closer to. In a decentralized setup, teams are better equipped to identify user needs and translate them into relevant Data Products. Centralized IT departments often struggle to capture these nuances, leading to solutions that may miss the mark in terms of consumer value.

Usability and readiness remain a challenge in both centralized and decentralized setups. In decentralized teams, Data Products are often highly tailored to the specific domain, which improves usability for that domain but limits reuse across the organization. In contrast, centralized teams may build more generic Data Products that aim to serve multiple domains, but these can lack the domain-specific refinements that drive real business value.

Reliability and transparency tend to be stronger in centralized setups. Central teams often include specialized roles, which makes it easier to ensure technical consistency, stability, and adherence to standards. Technical aspects such as monitoring, logging, and data governance are typically more mature in centralized teams, leading to greater operational reliability and auditability across Data Products.

Decentralized setups typically perform better when it comes to making Data Products understandable and self-describing. Since the teams building the Data Products are close to the business context, they know what the data represents and how it is used. This results in clearer naming, metadata, and documentation. In contrast, centralized teams often struggle with this aspect, as they lack deep domain knowledge, making it harder to describe the content and purpose of the Data Product effectively.

Decentralized units tend to maintain their Data Products more actively. Since the Data Product directly supports their own goals, there is a strong incentive to keep it accurate and up to date. Centralized teams, on the other hand, are often overloaded with competing priorities from multiple business units, which can delay updates or reduce responsiveness. As a result, Data Products owned centrally may lag in maintenance or approval cycles.

Centralized setups have a clear advantage when it comes to composability and interoperability. Guardrails such as shared data models, standardized interfaces, and common platforms can be effectively enforced from a central unit. This is especially important when Data Products are expected to interact with each other. In decentralized environments, differences in modeling standards, cloud platforms, or infrastructure (e.g., cross-cloud communication causing egress costs) often lead to incompatibilities and integration challenges.

Centralized setups generally perform better in ensuring trust, security, and reliability. They can afford to maintain specialized roles for data governance, privacy, and security; functions that are critical but often underrepresented in decentralized teams. Central units typically follow stricter compliance procedures and have better tooling to monitor data integrity and access control. While decentralized units also care about these aspects, they often lack the capacity or expertise to enforce them consistently across domains.

Centralized setups excel at making Data Products discoverable and addressable. With central coordination, organizations are more likely to enforce consistent standards for documentation, cataloging, and naming conventions. This makes it easier for teams to find and integrate existing Data Products across domains. In contrast, decentralized units often lack visibility into what other teams are building, leading to duplicated efforts and siloed solutions that are difficult to locate or consume.

Centralized setups are significantly better suited for ensuring a shared platform and consistent data modeling standards. They can enforce the use of common tools, data models, and cloud services across all teams. This reduces duplication, integration friction, and platform sprawl. In decentralized setups, teams often use different platforms, modeling conventions, or cloud providers, which leads to interoperability challenges and increased operational complexity.

Centralized setups are clearly superior when it comes to robustness. They typically maintain higher standards for testing, monitoring, and operational resilience, which is supported by specialized roles such as platform engineers, Site Reliability Engineers (SREs), and Quality Assurance experts. Decentralized teams often lack these dedicated capabilities, which can result in inconsistent levels of robustness across Data Products.

Neither centralized nor decentralized setups fully excel in managing data quality and integrity. Central teams are slightly better at enforcing consistent standards and quality frameworks across the organization. However, decentralized units have the advantage of understanding what quality means within their specific domain. A key limitation of central teams is their inability to define meaningful KPIs without domain context. This makes true data quality hard to enforce from a distance.

Centralized setups are significantly better equipped for ensuring monitoring and observability. With specialized roles, consistent tooling, and platform-level standards, they can establish robust monitoring across all Data Products. In contrast, decentralized teams often lack a shared understanding of how Data Products interconnect, making end-to-end observability difficult to achieve. As a result, blind spots and inconsistent metrics are common in decentralized models.

As shown above, there is no clear winner between centralized and decentralized setups. Each approach brings distinct advantages and trade-offs. Decentralized teams are typically closer to the business and therefore better at capturing domain-specific needs. However, they often lack the technical rigor, consistency, and governance structures of centralized models. Especially when it comes to data governance, the "G" in the GAP framework, both setups reveal significant weaknesses. While centralized models have a slight edge in terms of technical and operational excellence, this advantage is not decisive. The conclusion is clear: the best approach combines both worlds. In the next section, we'll explore how a hybrid model can harness the strengths of each setup while mitigating their downsides.

Hub and Spoke

Neither centralization nor decentralization has proven to be the definitive answer for building Data Products at scale. In practice, the most effective approach lies somewhere in between combining the strengths of both worlds. This is where the Hub-and-Spoke model comes into play.

The Hub-and-Spoke model leans slightly toward centralization but allows for decentralized flexibility, especially in areas like prioritization and data ownership. The Hub is typically a central unit (often within IT) that defines standards, sets guardrails, and operates shared platforms. The Spokes are the business units with technical capabilities. While they maintain a degree of independence, they are expected to comply with the standards defined by the Hub. This collaboration ensures that scalable Data Product development is possible without sacrificing domain relevance or governance.

In the heatmap in Figure 9, we outline the different responsibilities and where they typically fall: either in the Hub, the Spoke, or as a joint effort. While some areas have a clear ownership, others are more collaborative and require coordination between both sides.

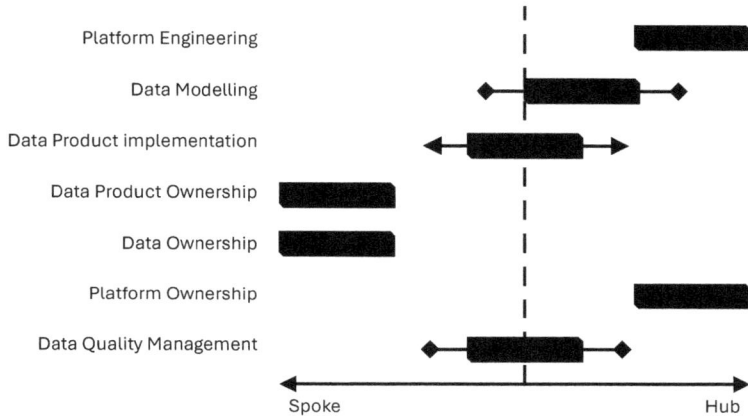

Figure 9: Responsibilities.

Before we explore each of the aspects in detail and reference the Data Product dimensions again, let's first clarify the meaning of the figure above. The boxes indicate where responsibility typically lies: either within the Hub, the Spoke, or both.

A box with arrows in both directions represents areas where responsibilities can reside in either unit, depending on the organization. Boxes with a diamond symbol highlight functions that require close collaboration between the Hub and Spoke to be effective. To improve clarity, this can also be translated into a RACI (Responsible, Accountable, Consulted, Informed) matrix, which clarifies roles and responsibilities across project tasks or processes.

Let's begin with Platform Engineering, a core function of the Hub. The Hub hosts dedicated engineering teams that ensure the platform powering the Data Products is stable, scalable, and ready to use. These teams build and maintain APIs that abstract away complexities such as data storage, access control, and infrastructure management. This ensures consistent guardrails across all Data Products.

The primary goal is to continuously improve the shared platform, increasing efficiency for all Data Products over time. Harmonization and standardization of tooling are key here. This setup directly supports several Data Product dimensions, including Reliability and Transparency, Composable and Interoperable, Trustworthiness and Security, Discoverability, Shared Models, and Robustness. It also contributes to cost efficiency, since a unified technological layer reduces licensing, data egress, and compute expenses.

The next key function is Data Modeling. While closely connected to the Platform Engineering team (since models often reuse shared APIs and tools), data modeling also requires deep business domain knowledge. Each domain model benefits greatly from input by business experts, making spoke involvement essential.

However, to ensure consistency across domain models and maintain technical alignment, the modeling function should be anchored in the Hub. The Hub provides the methodology, standards, and governance, while spoke representatives actively contribute to shaping the domain-specific content. For this collaboration to succeed, strong buy-in and continuous engagement from the spokes is critical, especially to ensure business relevance without compromising technical consistency.

This joint modeling setup supports a wide range of business-oriented Data Product dimensions, including clear purpose and consumer relevance, usability and readiness, reliability and transparency, understandable and self-describing, and approved and up to date. At the same time, it also reinforces key technical dimensions, such as composable and interoperable, discoverable and addressable, shared platform and models, as well as data quality and integrity management.

While this approach demands a higher level of alignment across teams, the Hub retains final accountability and decision-making authority. This ensures that decisions can be enforced effectively.

The third key aspect is Data Product implementation. Unlike platform or modeling responsibilities, there is no one-size-fits-all answer for where this function should reside; it strongly depends on the size and structure of the organization.

In smaller setups, a single Data Product team might cover the entire organization. In larger organizations, it's common to have dedicated teams embedded within each major business function. Alternatively, Data Product teams may be fully owned by the spokes but supported by shared resources from the Hub, like for technical support or architectural guidance.

This hybrid approach ensures that Data Products remain business-relevant, while still benefiting from centralized capabilities such as shared platforms, modeling standards, and common APIs. Close collaboration between the use-case teams and the Hub is essential to maintain alignment and avoid fragmentation.

The fourth key function is Data Product Ownership. Unlike the previous, more technical functions, this role focuses on the "what" rather than the "how." It is typically fully owned by the spokes, as they are in the business and best positioned to decide which Data Products to prioritize, which features to develop first, and how these align with business needs.

This prioritization process is closely tied to the framework discussed in Chapter four and can be applied at both the organizational level or within individual business units. The actual setup depends on factors such as team size, available budget, and strategic goals within each domain.

Like Data Product Ownership, Data Ownership lies clearly within the Spokes. Business units define what data quality means in their context and set the corresponding standards. This step is about defining expectations, not yet implementing them.

A decentralized approach to data ownership supports many key aspects of business-driven data products, such as clear purpose, usability, and relevance. It also contributes to several technical dimensions, particularly composable and interoperable, trustworthy and secure, discoverable, robust, and data quality management. This ensures that the data foundation is aligned with business needs from the start.

Platform ownership, in contrast, is fully anchored in the hub. The hub is responsible for making key decisions regarding the technology stack. This includes but is not limited to selecting cloud platforms, standardizing tooling, and managing software licenses. Centralizing these decisions avoids fragmentation across the organization, such as multiple reporting tools or competing data warehouse implementations.

A unified platform strategy requires a single authority with the mandate to enforce standards and ensure alignment. This promotes consistency, cost-efficiency, and interoperability. These are all key pillars for building scalable and composable Data Products.

Data quality management is a shared responsibility between the hub and the spokes. While data ownership is clearly located in the spokes, the implementation of data quality measures typically requires coordination across units and is often driven by the hub.

The hub plays a central role in embedding quality checks into platforms, APIs, and modeling workflows. It ensures that agreed-upon standards are consistently applied and that data quality is technically enforced where possible.

We will explore these implementation details in the upcoming sections. In practice, IT departments are frequently involved, as they have the ability to implement system-level checks and enforce data validity at the source and integration layers.

The Data Product team

A key question to address is how to structure a team capable of delivering one or more Data Products. While the previous section focused on embedding these responsibilities at an organizational level, this section explores the internal composition of a Data Product team.

Importantly, this is rarely a single, static team. Instead, it is typically a virtual team made up of several sub-teams and contributors from different functions. These are brought together to cover all required capabilities.

We will begin by identifying the core roles required for Data Product delivery and then discuss how they can be organized effectively.

Roles for Data Products

Before we investigate the team structure, it is important to define the roles involved in delivering a Data Product. While technical roles such as data engineers, data architects, or data scientists are commonly known and widely documented, this section focuses on the less obvious roles. Roles that are equally critical for success but often overlooked in traditional team compositions.

Data product owner

A central role in every Data Product team is the data product owner. This role is typically embedded in a business unit and is responsible for defining the vision, managing the roadmap, and prioritizing features based on business value. The data product owner holds final accountability for the success of the Data Product and acts as the key decision-maker. Depending on the organization's size and structure, one person may own multiple Data Products. While the data product owner works closely with the delivery team, they usually report into a business function and not into the Data or IT organization.

Squad lead

The Squad lead is responsible for the operational coordination of the Data Product. This role is similar to a scrum master, focusing on translating the priorities set by the data product owner into concrete tasks and ensuring they are effectively distributed among the technical team members. While the data product owner defines the vision and strategic direction, the squad lead ensures smooth execution and day-to-day progress. It's important to note that this is not a people management role. The squad lead has no formal leadership responsibility over team members, but instead ensures that the team is aligned and the Data Product delivery stays on track.

Proxy data product owner

For more complex Data Products, it can be helpful to introduce a proxy data product owner. While this role is not required in every setup, it serves an important function: bridging the gap between the business-focused Data Product Owner and the technical delivery team. The proxy role often brings in the necessary technical understanding that the primary product owner may lack or may not have the time to apply fully due to other responsibilities. Positioned closer to the delivery team, the proxy product owner ensures that the strategic vision is effectively translated into actionable tasks.

Data product tech lead

Every Data Product team requires a strong tech lead. This role is focused on ensuring the technical success of the product. The tech lead has deep expertise in the technologies used and is well-versed in both the GAP model (as described in Chapter 2) and the DRIVE framework introduced in Chapter 3. The tech lead may not always be dedicated full-time to a single team; often, they support multiple Data Products depending on complexity and team size. Their main responsibilities include enforcing technical standards, guiding implementation best practices, and ensuring that tools and platforms are used effectively and consistently across the team.

Chapter leads

A formal reporting structure is introduced through the chapter leads. While they do not have an active delivery role within a Data Product team, they are responsible for managing the people (typically engineers) who contribute to those teams. Chapter leads focus on people development, including upskilling, mentoring, and ensuring the right capabilities are available across squads. Although they stay out of daily technical decisions, they should have a solid understanding of the technologies their teams work with. This role is essential to decouple people management from technical delivery, promoting both organizational clarity and team performance. In larger organizations, multiple chapter leads may exist to cover different skill domains.

Engineering roles for data retrieval and integration

Each Data Product team has different roles to match the DRIVE framework. This includes the data engineers, data modelers, platform engineers, data product reliability engineer (similar to a Site Reliability Engineer or SRE for short), data governance leads, and data stewards.

Roles for value extraction

There are different roles for value extraction, such as the analytical engineers, BI developers, AI engineers, or data scientists, that complement the data product team.

Organizational setup

Now that the key roles have been defined, we can examine how these roles are structured into teams. For this purpose, we use the Spotify model[3] as a reference, as it offers agility and flexibility. These qualities are highly beneficial when applied to Data Product delivery.

As outlined in the previous section, we distinguish between operational responsibility for Data Product delivery and staff management responsibilities. This separation brings multiple advantages: chapter leads can focus on developing talent and skills, while squad leads concentrate on execution. This avoids the common bottlenecks found in traditional organizations, where overloaded team leads often slow down delivery. It also creates flexibility to dynamically assign engineers to high-priority initiatives as needed.

A squad is a virtual team composed of members from both the business side (spokes) and the centralized units (hub), where the chapters are located. In addition, there are typically dedicated platforms and API teams responsible for building and maintaining the shared infrastructure. As organizational maturity increases, the size of these shared teams tends to decrease.

---

[3] Spotify Model:
   https://www.researchgate.net/publication/352713951_An_architecture_governance_a
   pproach_for_Agile_development_by_tailoring_the_Spotify_model/link/60d56324299
   bf1ea9ebad22a/download.

Similarly, modeling teams are responsible for ensuring consistent data models across domains. In mature setups, these teams are often embedded into the squads themselves.

Figure 10 illustrates how such a setup can be visualized.

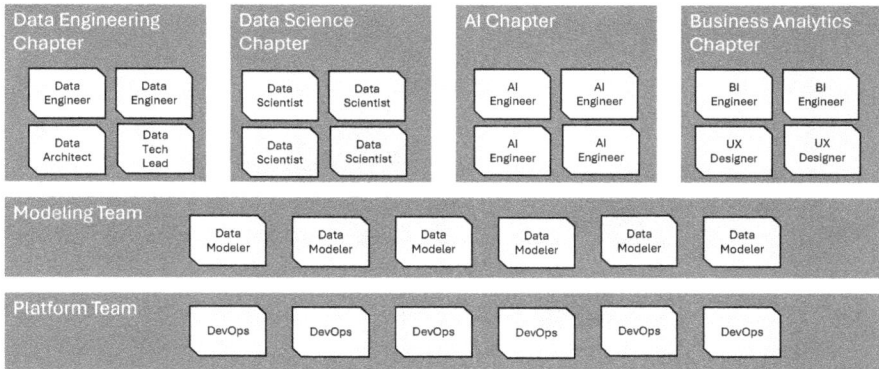

Figure 10: The squad.

It is important to note that this structure serves merely as an illustration. The actual number and type of chapters may vary depending on the size and maturity of the organization. Both the modeling team and platform team are typically organized as chapters. As organizational maturity increases, members of these teams are gradually embedded into the squads.

In less mature setups, especially during the initial development of data models or platform services, these teams often operate independently of the squads to accelerate foundational work. Finally, not all roles are depicted in this simplified diagram. In practice, the setup is usually more comprehensive and may involve additional functions.

The next step is the formation of a data product squad. This squad is a virtual team assembled to work on one or more Data Products. It does not follow a fixed reporting line but instead brings together roles and functions from various chapters and business units. The composition is flexible and based on the specific needs of the Data Product.

Figure 11 outlines how such a virtual squad can be structured.

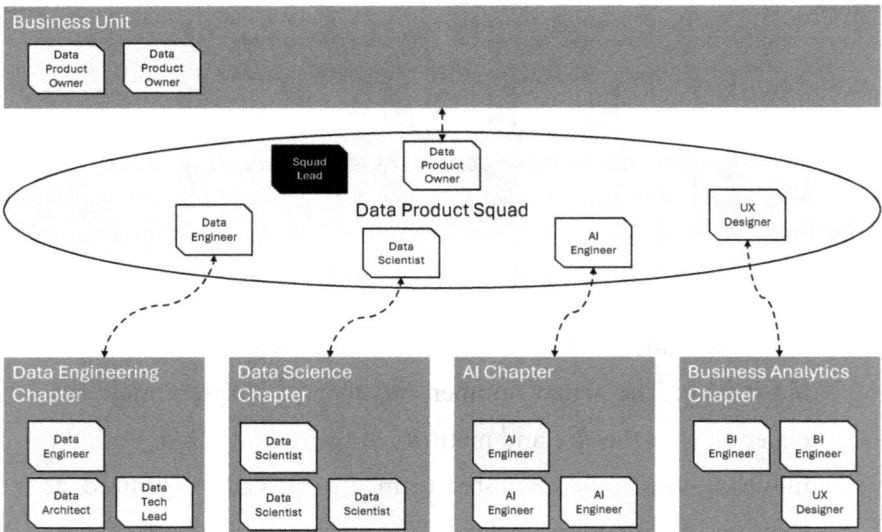

Figure 11: Virtual squad.

While the model presented serves as a blueprint, it can be adapted to the specific needs of each enterprise. Chapter sizes typically range between 15 and 40 people and focus on developing deep expertise in areas like AI, data engineering, or analytics. This allows the squads to concentrate on product delivery rather than people development. Chapters can also combine internal and external talent, including near- and offshore capabilities, offering both flexibility and scalability. With this structure in place, organizations can ensure a strong balance between operational agility and technical excellence.

Having covered the organizational and business aspects of Data Products, we will now continue our journey through the DRIVE framework in the upcoming chapters.

Key learnings

- **Decentral versus central**: The benefits and downsides of both setups were discussed.

- **Hub and spoke**: A setup that takes the best out of both worlds – from decentral and central setups.

- **Roles in a Data Product team**: discussion of the most important roles, such as the Data Product owner.

- **Organizing your Data Product team**: How to work in an agile setup with chapters and squads.

The Technical Dimension

Part III is focused on the technical aspects of Data Products. In the next three chapters, we will get an overview of the most important tools and techniques that are essential to build them. This part serves as a toolbox for your future work on Data Products.

Six

Retrieval

Excel.

Data often starts with Excel. And too often, it ends with it.

It's the fragile backbone of far too many so-called "Data Products." In reality, Excel isn't just a tool. It's a quiet saboteur. A silent dependency that gives data executives sleepless nights, even if they don't know why. It's easy, familiar, and everywhere, and precisely because of that, it's dangerous.

I once witnessed a failure that shows exactly what's wrong with relying on fragile ingestion pipelines. A quarterly reporting workflow was based on a simple but brittle process: someone exported data from SAP, saved it as Excel, and emailed it to a data engineer. That engineer would upload the file manually, triggering the pipeline that processed the report. This shaky setup worked for a few quarters, until both people were sick at the same time.

The pipeline broke. No one noticed until the CFO saw that his cash flow report was missing. This wasn't just any report. It was his signature dashboard. And yet, it was running on a process that involved manual Excel exports and untracked email attachments. The cost for a proper SAP connector had been deemed "too high." But the real cost came later, when the whole thing crashed and burned.

And that's what this chapter is about.

We'll now look at how to avoid exactly these kinds of failures by building reliable, scalable, and maintainable data ingestion strategies. You'll learn how to bring data from different data-producing systems into your platform in a structured way. We'll cover real-time versus batch ingestion, common challenges with change data capture, and the principles of building ingestion pipelines that are resilient from day one. This is the foundation, the first step in the DRIVE framework, and the entry point for any Data Product.

This chapter provides a high-level overview of the topic of data retrieval. It is intentionally limited in scope, as this topic could easily fill an entire book on its own. The goal in this chapter is to introduce the core concepts and create a solid foundation.

Let's fix ingestion for good.

Strategies for acquiring data: Streaming versus Batch

A fundamental decision in data retrieval is whether to ingest data in batch or streaming mode. While real-time delivery is often seen as more expensive, batch ingestion comes with inherent latency, making data less timely. However, this trade-off is not always a matter of choice since many legacy systems only support batch exports. This limits the architectural flexibility.

Both real-time and near-real-time architectures rely on streaming patterns and can evolve incrementally. In a streaming setup, data is processed continuously in small increments and made available to downstream systems immediately. This reduces load spikes at specific times (such as month-end) and flattens data volume over time, enabling more predictable infrastructure scaling.

From a business perspective, streaming enables more responsive Data Products: decisions are made with fresher data, issues are detected earlier, and operations become more agile. A critical enabler of streaming ingestion is Change Data Capture (CDC).

That said, streaming is not always feasible. Many existing systems, especially in enterprise environments, lack real-time integration capabilities. In such cases, traditional ETL-based batch ingestion remains necessary. This chapter will address both approaches and highlight best practices to ensure robust, scalable ingestion, regardless of system maturity.

Streaming Data: Change Data Capture (CDC) as a basis

Before implementing streaming-based data retrieval, one essential question must be answered: Is the data-producing system capable of delivering real-time data? Not all systems are. Many emit data only periodically, for example, once per day or per hour. In such cases, building a real-time Data Product with sub-second latency offers no added value and only increases complexity and cost.

In general, the frequency of data changes should guide the architectural choice. High-volume sources like clickstreams from webshops generate data continuously and benefit greatly from streaming architectures. In contrast, information such as a customer's email address changes infrequently and doesn't create a high load on your streaming infrastructure. When was the last time you changed your e-mail address? Exactly, we don't need highly scalable processing for that.

One of the most powerful techniques in streaming-based ingestion is Change Data Capture (CDC). With CDC, only records that have changed are transmitted. This reduces the need to reload entire datasets. Consider the following example: a customer updates her profile, stating she now works at a large law firm instead of being a student. This detail may trigger new product recommendations or marketing campaigns. In a batch-based process, this update may not appear until the end of the month, when all customer records are reprocessed. With CDC, the change is captured and propagated in near real-time, often within kilobytes in size per message, enabling immediate action and reducing processing overhead.

We can design CDC-enabled architectures for new systems by applying the outbox pattern, which is well-suited for event-driven environments. For legacy systems, where direct change tracking is often not possible, we can use alternative techniques to enable CDC. These approaches will be discussed in detail throughout this section.

The outbox pattern for CDC

One of the most effective strategies for enabling CDC in Data Products is the outbox pattern. This approach ensures that every time data within an application is created, updated, or deleted, a corresponding change event is generated. These events are stored in an outbox table, where our Data Product can now consume the changes.

The outbox pattern is particularly common in microservice architectures and newly developed applications. Once emitted, these change events can be consumed by downstream pipelines, which update the target data stores that power the Data Products. This enables near-real-time synchronization between operational systems and analytical or serving layers, without tight coupling.

Figure 12 shows how the outbox pattern works in practice:

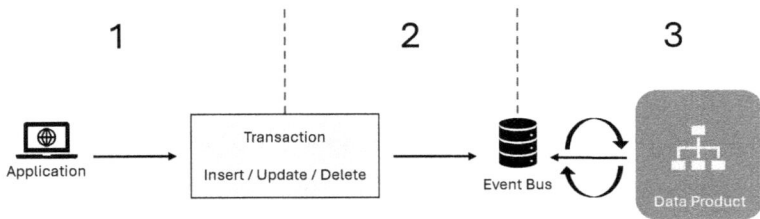

Figure 12: The outbox pattern.

Basically, there are some key steps involved in this pattern:

- **Step 1**: A user interacts with the application and triggers a data change, such as creating, updating, or deleting a record. This change is written to the application's database as part of a transaction.

- **Step 2**: As part of the same transaction, a corresponding change event is written to an outbox table on an Event Bus (e.g., Apache Kafka). The outbox table acts as a reliable interface for downstream consumers.

- **Step 3**: The Data Product reads from the outbox table, either continuously (real-time) or in batches at defined intervals. Once an event has been processed, it is marked accordingly, ensuring idempotency and traceability. The change is then persisted in the Data Product's target storage, keeping it up to date.

This approach offers several key advantages, making it one of the most effective strategies for Change Data Capture. First, it reduces the load on the data-producing application, since there is no need for frequent polling or batch-based ETL jobs to check for changes. Second, it eliminates the need to directly access the producer's database, which improves system decoupling and respects the boundaries of application ownership. Third, it enables near-real-time updates, significantly reducing latency and allowing Data Products to reflect the latest state with minimal delay.

Additionally, because the events are created as part of the application's transaction, data consistency is guaranteed. There is no risk of missing or partially applied updates. The clear separation of write and read responsibilities also improves system resilience and simplifies error handling. Finally, this pattern scales well across microservices and supports event-driven architectures, enabling Data Products to be both highly responsive and loosely coupled to operational systems.

Other CDC strategies

Not all use cases can be solved with the outbox pattern described in the previous section. That approach works best when we control the development of the source application or can influence its implementation. But in reality, many data sources lie outside our control. They may come from third-party systems, legacy applications, or managed cloud services. In such cases, there are lighter alternatives to traditional ETL-based ingestion.

One of the most common options is to leverage database-level change logs, often referred to as Write-Ahead Logs (WALs) or Change Streams. These transaction logs record changes made to the database and can be used to identify insertions, updates, or deletions. To tap into these logs, we need specialized frameworks such as Debezium, which listen to change events and publish them to a message bus. This enables real-time or near-real-time data propagation.

While this approach introduces some additional load on the source database, it is typically much more efficient than running frequent full-scale ETL jobs. It is especially effective when the underlying databases are owned or managed internally. Figure 13 illustrates how this architecture works.

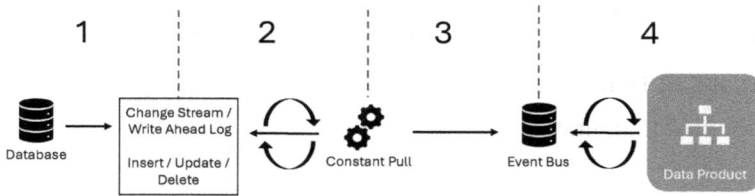

Figure 13: Adding the WAL.

As shown in the image, this approach introduces an additional layer of complexity compared to the outbox pattern: we need to continuously read from the database's change stream or write-ahead log (WAL). This does introduce some overhead on the source database, but the impact is usually limited, as these logs are typically decoupled from the operational workload. Mature frameworks like Debezium help reduce the implementation effort, offering pre-built connectors for popular databases.

We won't go into every detail of the figure here, as the downstream processing remains largely identical to the outbox pattern: events are published, consumed, and stored in the Data Product's underlying infrastructure. This approach is also well-suited for older systems, and we can gather data from some legacy systems.

When neither the outbox pattern nor a change stream–based approach can be applied, there is still one more option to retrieve data in near real time for Data Products. However, this method should be considered a last resort and used only in exceptional cases. For completeness, we add the trigger-based CDC approach here as well.

Most databases support triggers. These are small routines that execute when specific events, such as insert, update, or delete, occur. These triggers can be configured to write to an outbox table, similar to the pattern described earlier. However, this approach comes with significant trade-offs: triggers add processing overhead, and the more of them you implement, the greater the impact on the performance and stability of operational systems. For this reason, trigger-based CDC should only be used for specialized scenarios, where no other approach is feasible and the operational risks are well understood. Please use this approach with caution.

Batch load: Ingest strategies

The traditional way of retrieving data is through batch ingestion. This is a common pattern for many use cases when building a Data Product. In many situations, data producers do not enable CDC at the source, as described in the previous section, so we need to retrieve the data in batches from the producing systems.

Several aspects must be considered here. The first is the interval of the data loads. We need to determine when and for what purpose the data is required. This can range from hourly to daily or even monthly loads. Another important consideration is timing. Batch retrieval often generates a significant load on the databases that power production systems. Therefore, it must be carefully planned to avoid impacting business operations. A common approach is to run the loads at night, when system usage is typically lower.

In addition, many SaaS solutions only provide data access via batch loading, since they usually do not support real-time queries. A typical pattern here is to query their APIs via RESTful web requests.

Full versus incremental loads

A key consideration at the very beginning is whether the load will be full or incremental. In some cases, it may be necessary to load the entire database of a production system into the data platform that supports our Data Product. However, the cost of doing so is very high, as it involves moving large volumes of data between the production system and the data platform. This results in significant compute costs and network egress, especially in cloud environments. Still, there are scenarios where this is the only viable option. These scenarios are mainly relevant in legacy systems that allow no other option.

With full loads, we can either replace all data each time or implement an algorithm to calculate deltas and update only the changed records. Both approaches are challenging, though various tools exist to support them. In my experience, many of the most severe failures and system issues have originated from these types of loads.

A more efficient approach is to use incremental loads, where only new or changed data is added. The concept is similar to previously discussed patterns, but instead of tracking individual changes, we focus on all data that has changed since the last retrieval. This reduces system load but may require a delta mechanism to be implemented. Most SaaS applications simplify this by exposing APIs that return data in delta chunks, either as files or API responses. Also, tools such as Airbyte support cursorless queries that kind of load.

This approach introduces an additional complexity: in data warehouses, incoming data often needs to be processed in a specific order, especially when pre- and post-processing steps are required. To handle this, we will learn about the concept of DAGs later in this chapter. Also, connecting to multiple sources might create complexity for data engineers. The role of data engineers typically isn't one that is easy to hire, so it is necessary to take offload from them. There are numerous open source and commercial tools that ease the data ingestion, such as Data Load Tool (dlt), Airbyte, or Fivetran.

File-based load

A common approach for data ingestion is file-based loading. This is similar to what we discussed earlier. Many systems that produce data periodically offload deltas as files. One key benefit is that this method imposes minimal load on the source systems, as it is often built in. On the receiving end, which powers our Data Products, it also offers the advantage of ingesting only the changed data.

Most of the time, the data arrives as CSV exports, which are often poorly structured. However, many databases are equipped with built-in mechanisms to handle and properly load these files. More advanced systems may offload data in formats like XML or JSON, which offer additional flexibility in structure, including support for arrays and other complex types.

A key challenge in this approach is ensuring proper data quality. It is essential to check for metadata in the producing systems. Ideally, a metadata file is sent alongside the data files, providing relevant information for validation. Files delivered to a landing zone can then be processed by a batch load job that periodically ingests them.

Robust error-handling mechanisms are crucial in this setup. Files might be delivered multiple times in case of processing errors, and they may contain missing or corrupt data.

In principle, this approach works well, but it requires extensive validation checks to be effective. In many cases, these checks were implemented with limited effort, leading to significant issues in data handling systems. While file ingestion is typically easy to set up and offers a high degree of flexibility, it can also create numerous challenges if not executed properly.

Timestamp-based load

Another option for retrieving deltas from systems is timestamp-based loading. This approach is partially considered a CDC technique, as it relies on the database assigning a timestamp to each record when it is created or modified. The data retrieval job then compares this timestamp to the time of the last successful run. If the timestamp is more recent, the record is considered updated and needs to be processed.

This method typically operates on a row level, meaning that either the entire row is replaced, or additional logic must be implemented to identify what exactly has changed within the row.

A key challenge here is late-arriving data. If a retrieval job runs for two hours, changes can occur during that window, especially to rows queried at the start.

Consider this workflow: a CRM stores customer purchases. A linking table holds order IDs and their customer; a separate order-details table lists the products per order. The job first collects all changed order IDs, then fetches their details. If the job runs long, new changes can land mid-run: an order may appear in the linking table after we scanned it, while its details are captured later when we query the details table. We end up with a complete set of line items for an order, but no customer association, simply because updates arrived out of sequence during the job.

This is not rare; it's a common source of inconsistency that keeps data engineers up at night.

Full load

When delta mechanisms or CDC are unavailable, the fallback is a full load. This should be a last resort because it is costly for both the source systems and the target platform. Transfers often involve gigabytes to terabytes of data, creating significant load; compute, network bandwidth, and egress costs can escalate quickly.

Such retrieval jobs typically run overnight or during periods of low activity on the source systems' primary workloads. Detecting what has changed is complex, as every row may need to be compared. Sometimes replacing all data would be simpler, but downstream logic often makes this impractical. Also, we have the same issue as before with the late-arriving data. In full loads, this gets even more complicated as the jobs run typically longer.

This approach should only be used when there is no other option, and it can be used for data with low volume.

Important concepts for data retrieval

Directed acyclic graphs (DAGs)

A commonly used technique for data retrieval is the directed acyclic graph (DAG). DAGs help structure workflows by clearly defining dependencies between individual steps. The key principle is that the workflow must not contain any cycles. Each task can only depend on tasks that come before it, ensuring a clear and logical execution order.

Imagine this scenario: your Data Product needs to load data from three systems: CRM, Claims, and Controlling. The goal is to calculate the number of new customers per day and display it in a dashboard. See Figure 14.

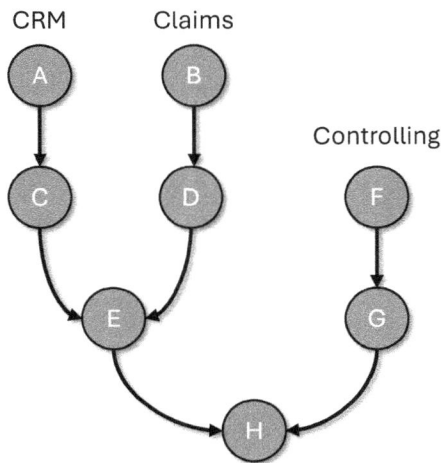

Figure 14: DAG example.

The CRM system contains all sales data. The Claims system shows which products were returned. To calculate the net number of new customers, we retrieve the sales data from CRM (step A) and transform this data (step C). In parallel, we do the same for the Claims data (steps B and D). Next, we subtract the returns from the Claims data (step E).

In parallel to this, we load the data from the controlling system and transform it accordingly (steps F and H). The validation against the controlling system happens in step H. This workflow ensures that all steps are executed before we get to step H.

Since each step depends on the previous one, the process must follow a strict order to ensure correct results. If not, we might miss the claims data and end up calculating an incorrect number of new customers. This quickly leads to disputes with business units, a discussion the data team is typically not well-equipped to win.

We won't go into the full theory of DAGs here, but it's helpful to mention the key aspects: a DAG consists of nodes or vertices (in our case, the round boxes labeled with each step) and directed connections between them, called edges. The core principle is that a DAG must not contain any cycles. This ensures that the workflow eventually reaches an end when the job is complete.

There are many solutions available for implementing DAGs, such as Apache Airflow or Dagster. We won't go into tooling details here, as this will be covered in Volume two of the book series. Also, it is essential to mention that DAGs are not only relevant for this phase (data retrieval) but also in the next step (integration).

Ensuring quality in the data retrieval phase

Whatever we get right at the beginning of a Data Product's journey has a significant impact on the outcome. If we fail early on, the challenges only grow larger later. But Data quality is not just a technical concern; there are broader aspects involved. One of the key enablers of quality isn't more tools or processes. It starts with people. In this section, we will provide an overview of the topics of quality. With the GAP triad introduced in Chapter 2, it isn't treated as a separate domain. It is essential to do it in the entire journey of each Data Product.

Data Quality is a people's business

Data quality starts at the very beginning, and that means the data entry phase. Even before we retrieve data, we need to focus on how it is initially created.

Take this example: imagine a POS system used by shop employees. These employees are under pressure during customer interactions, and entering clean, structured data is rarely their top priority. In fact, many see it as a tedious task. But data quality doesn't start with automated transformations. It starts with building systems that guide users toward correct data entry. The interface and workflow must support accuracy and ease of use from the outset.

Beyond system design, awareness is key. People working in data-producing roles (essentially across all business units) need to understand the importance of what they enter. I once worked with a call center team where we had almost no insight into the reasons for incoming calls. We were spending heavily on outsourced services, but the perceived quality remained poor. Without clear data, we couldn't explain why people kept calling. This was before automated AI transcripts existed.

When we investigated, the root cause became obvious: call center agents were measured by average handling time and the number of calls processed. Logging call reasons didn't help them hit their targets; it hurt them. While we didn't succeed in changing the KPIs, we conducted training sessions and improved the software to reduce the number of selectable options. Within a few months, data quality improved significantly. We finally understood why people were calling and we could act on that insight, which led to substantial cost savings.

The lesson is clear: to achieve high data quality, start at the source. Train people to enter data correctly and build systems that make doing the right thing the easy thing. Organizations need to invest in data literacy and change management. Small improvements early in the data journey have a huge impact later, especially when it comes to the value delivered by a Data Product.

Failing to invest in people working with systems will create a lot of headaches afterwards. This topic is often neglected but has a huge impact. Small investments here bring a lot of savings afterwards. This is why a Data Product isn't just about the technology; it is an end-to-end thinking of how we get there. Needless to say, it starts with people.

Metadata collection from the very beginning

The most important information about our data comes from the systems that produce it. What users are allowed to enter in these systems is a crucial source for collecting metadata, as it often reflects embedded business logic. Capturing this business logic should begin from day one.

This metadata is stored in a data catalog to describe the data across different layers. There are many metadata catalog tools available, but we won't discuss them here as they're largely commoditized. Instead, we will focus on the types of metadata that should be collected:

- **Descriptive Metadata**: This type of metadata describes the content of the data itself. For example, take a field named "fname". Without metadata, it's unclear whether this stands for "first name" or "full name." Descriptive metadata provides clarity: a possible description could be, "The full name of the customer. It starts with the first name, may include a middle name, and ends with the last name." With descriptive metadata, it becomes clear what the data represents.

- **Technical Metadata**: This refers to the technical characteristics required to process the data. For example, the compression algorithm used, source system, file type, or character encoding. This metadata supports efficient and correct data handling in downstream Data Products and reduces effort for engineers working with the data.

- **Administrative Metadata**: This covers the administrative aspects of the data, such as data owner(s), access rights, and legal constraints such as copyrights. It is essential to know who to contact and under what conditions the data can be accessed or used.

- **Structural Metadata**: This describes how different data assets are related to each other. It helps identify dependencies and informs how various parts of the data should be integrated or processed.

Proper metadata management from the very beginning is essential to ensure that our Data Products meet the quality standards expected by end users. Getting this right is critical. Without it, we risk failing to deliver reliable outcomes. And once that happens, trust from consumers quickly erodes.

Data contracts as enablers for data quality

A key aspect of data quality is having a clear understanding of what data can enter the Data Product, under what conditions, and how to identify when data is faulty or corrupted. This is where Data Contracts come into play: they define exactly these boundaries and expectations.

A data contract is an agreement between a data producer and a data consumer. It specifies the format, type, and schema of the data, along with the rules that determine whether the data is valid. This alignment ensures both sides understand what the other needs and what can be expected.

Data contracts can be implemented at various stages of the data retrieval process described earlier. One of the most common approaches is using schemas in messaging middleware. For example, Apache Kafka supports schema registries that define how data must be structured when published to a topic. Other tools provide similar capabilities for different types of data retrieval pipelines.

While there are emerging standards such as the Open Data Contract Standard from the Linux Foundation, most tools still use their own schema definitions, and implementations must be adapted accordingly. Data contracts are an essential concept, though still in the early stages of adoption, and the ecosystem around them is evolving rapidly.

However, there are several core elements that every data contract should contain:

- **Basic elements**: Includes general information such as the title, version, and a description of the data contract.

- **Schema**: Defines the structure of the dataset: what fields are present, their data types and formats, and whether they are nullable.

- **Data quality rules**: Specifies constraints related to data quality, such as, but not limited to, valid ranges for numeric values, acceptable date spans, or minimum and maximum row counts. These rules can be flexibly defined depending on the use case.

Data contracts help ensure high-quality data ingestion and align expectations between producers and consumers. They are typically written in YAML, making them both flexible and extensible. For every new Data Product, implementing a Data Contract should be considered essential.

We won't go into detailed implementations or schema definitions here, as that would go beyond the scope of this book.

Another important aspect is testing your data. In many situations, it is not possible to implement data contracts. This is especially true when working with older systems. Greenfield applications make it easy to build data contracts from the start. But legacy systems often cannot support that approach.

In these cases, data testing becomes essential. Tools like Great Expectations or Soda help with this. They let you define rules for your data. You can test for things like missing values, wrong formats, or unexpected changes. These tests run automatically and alert you when something goes wrong. This helps you maintain trust in your Data Products.

Key learnings

- **Streaming versus batch**: what are the benefits of each, and when to use what.

- **CDC**: Change Data Capture as a key building block of data retrieval for Data Products—what it is and why it is important.

- **DAGs**: how directed acyclic graphs contribute to a sustainable data retrieval function.

- **Qualitative aspects**: Data Quality at the very start of each Data Product.

SEVEN

Integration

I was hired to supercharge the company's data strategy. The board director's ambition and promises to the business were high. He sold the vision well, and he sold me the job. One of the largest financial institutions in Central and Eastern Europe, active in over ten countries, with strong returns. It sounded exciting.

Day one told a different story. The company had the simplest data model imaginable: none. No model, no problems, until regulations like IFRS 17 loomed. AI and analytics engineers in businesses had nothing trustworthy to work with.

With a small, ambitious team of eight, we started from scratch. We built roadmaps, architectures, strategies, and executable use cases. We aligned stakeholders, scored use cases by impact and cost, and prepared thoroughly for the budget meeting. Support was secured; buy-in was strong.

Then things shifted. A legacy project, running for five years already, was severely delayed and would consume a high double-digit amount in the millions next year. There was "no way back," and it took priority. Funding for everything else disappeared.

I was frustrated: no data models, no data science, no AI. The business would have to wait at least two years. Needless to say, this marked the beginning of my exit from the company.

This chapter is the logical next step after data retrieval: data modeling. We'll cover the layered Medallion architecture and core modeling strategies. As with the previous chapter, this is an overview. This topic could fill an entire book, so we'll focus on the golden path from raw data to reliable models.

Strategies for data integration

A solid data model is the foundation for success in AI. It provides end users with meaningful, usable data and helps build trust in the results. In this chapter, we'll explore several technologies and techniques. We'll begin with a layered approach, which serves as a flexible foundation for the modeling strategies that follow.

We've already discussed the types of Data Products earlier in the book, where we learned about source-aligned, aggregated, and consumer-aligned Data Products. While they describe the target audience, we will focus here on the inner workings of a Data

Product. One approach is to layer a Data Product with the Medallion architecture. Other concepts exist as well, but this is very popular and has all the ingredients needed to build a working Data Product. There are two approaches to building a Medallion architecture: either inside the Data Product or outside of it (with a joint layer for consistency). We won't dive into this, as this is a matter of concrete implementation. In this section, we will look at the overall theory of it.

Medallion architecture

Building your data using the Medallion architecture is a strong starting point. It offers a high degree of flexibility and makes it clear from the beginning which stage the data is in. The architecture is named after its three key processing layers: Bronze, Silver, and Gold—thus medallion. In each layer, the data is transformed and enriched progressively. Figure 15 illustrates this structure.

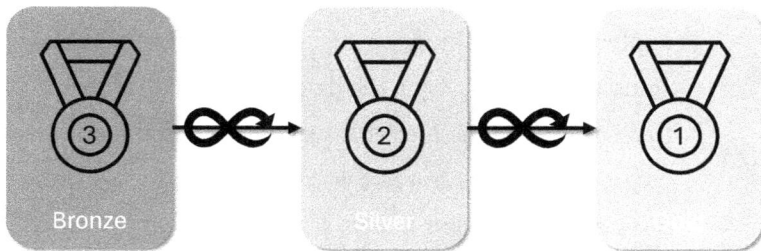

Figure 15: Medallion architecture.

Each layer in the Medallion architecture represents a different level of data maturity. Bronze is closest to the source system, while

Gold contains refined data that is most useful for business users. This serves as the final layer in our Data Product. The key idea is to decouple different requirements on the data and ensure that (re)processing can happen at any time without disrupting downstream usage. Let's briefly explore each layer:

- **Bronze**: The Bronze layer contains data exactly as it was retrieved. Raw and unmodified, staying as close as possible to the structure produced by the source systems. Some minimal additions may occur, such as metadata fields indicating when the data arrived, but no transformations are applied. This layer serves primarily as a staging area for downstream processing and provides the ability to reprocess data if needed. It follows the initial validation against data contracts, meaning the data here meets a basic quality threshold as defined by those contracts.

- **Silver**: The Silver layer contains data that has undergone initial processing. This includes cleaning, validation, and applying quality checks to ensure the data meets defined standards. At this stage, the data is typically transformed to align with a data model. Silver data is suitable for technical use cases but not yet ready for end users or business consumption.

- **Gold**: The Gold layer is the final stage. This is the stage presented to end users of the Data Product. It contains fully transformed data that is ready for business consumption. This layer incorporates extensive business logic and serves as the foundation for the business-facing Data Product itself, whether it's a report, the output of a data science model, an API, or an LLM. Essentially, the Gold layer is what end users interact with. It's the data for the visible part of the Data Product.

Important to mention here is to state clearly that Medallion is an architecture, not a modeling strategy. It is about how the data progresses through each layer. How the data is modeled in each of the layers is a completely other discipline – one we will explore in the next sections.

Normalization and denormalization

A key topic in modern database design is the trade-off between normalization and denormalization. While normalization is optimized for write performance and is commonly used in operational systems like CRMs, denormalization prioritizes read performance, making it more suitable for analytics.

Normalized data follows a set of rules in relational database design aimed at reducing redundancy and ensuring data integrity. The most common approach is Third Normal Form (3NF). In a normalized model, data is split into related tables based on logical groupings.

Let's return to our car analogy. See Figure 16.

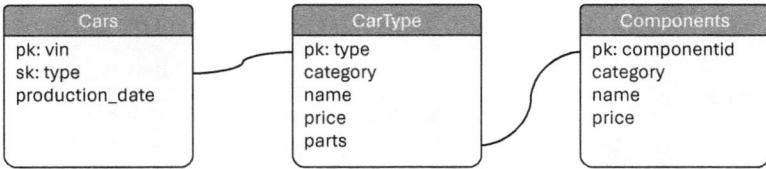

Figure 16: Normalization example.

This is a simplified example, intended to illustrate the basic principles of normalization. In this schema, data can be efficiently updated. For example, changing the price of a component doesn't affect other tables, as the structure relies on clearly defined relationships. However, this structure poses challenges for analytics. Suppose we want to calculate the manufacturing cost of a car versus its selling price. In a normalized model, such analytical queries become complex and expensive because the structure is optimized for writing data, not for reading or aggregating it. Figure 17 shows how a denormalized structure could address this.

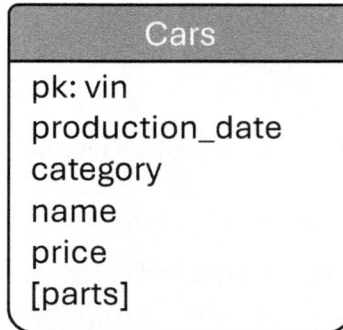

Figure 17: Denormalization example.

In this simplified example, we've pulled everything into a single table and used an array to represent the parts. This allows us to retrieve the price of all components with a single query, significantly improving query performance since no joins are required. However, this speed comes at a cost: data redundancy. Every car record now holds its own copy of the component data. If we need to update the price of a component used in 1,000 cars, we have to update it 1,000 times instead of just once, as we would in a normalized structure.

While the example is simplified, the takeaway is clear: both approaches have distinct advantages and trade-offs, depending on the use case.

During the lifecycle of a Data Product, we typically encounter both forms of data modeling. Data often arrives from source systems in a normalized form. However, to build algorithms and deliver business value, we need to transform this data into a denormalized format. Different approaches use a different level of denormalization versus normalization, which we will explore in the next section of the book.

In the Bronze layer, data is source-driven, which is often in a normalized structure. As we move to Silver and Gold, the data becomes increasingly denormalized. These layers are optimized for read-heavy use cases.

Star schema and snowflake schema

The easiest way to model data for analytical purposes is by using a star schema. This approach follows a denormalized design and is optimized for efficient querying. At its core, the star schema consists of a fact table at the center, surrounded by dimension tables that are referenced by the fact table.

This structure is easy to understand and query, as it reduces complexity and minimizes the number of required joins. Figure 18 illustrates this using our car manufacturer example:

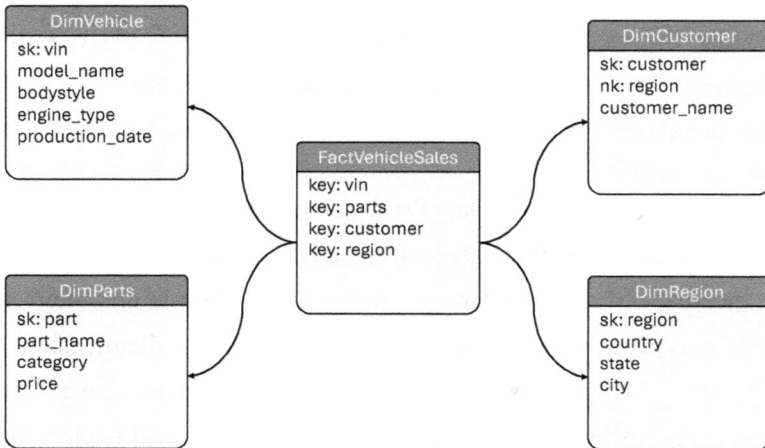

Figure 18: Star schema example.

In our example, the fact table represents the vehicle sales. From this central fact, we can establish relationships to key dimensions, such as the vehicle sold, the parts used, the customer, and the region. This setup enables straightforward queries, like analyzing sales by region or calculating the cost of a car based on its components.

The key advantage of this approach is minimizing the number of joins per query. In contrast to highly normalized structures, fewer joins mean better performance in read-intensive scenarios.

Another approach to modeling data for analytical purposes is the Snowflake schema. It is similar to the star schema but introduces more complexity by normalizing the dimension tables. In a Snowflake schema, a dimension can have its own sub-dimensions. This results in additional tables and relationships.

This makes the Snowflake schema more complex than the star schema, and queries typically involve more joins. However, for certain scenarios with complex enterprise logic, the star schema alone may not be sufficient.

In our car manufacturer example, a Snowflake schema might look like what appears in Figure 19

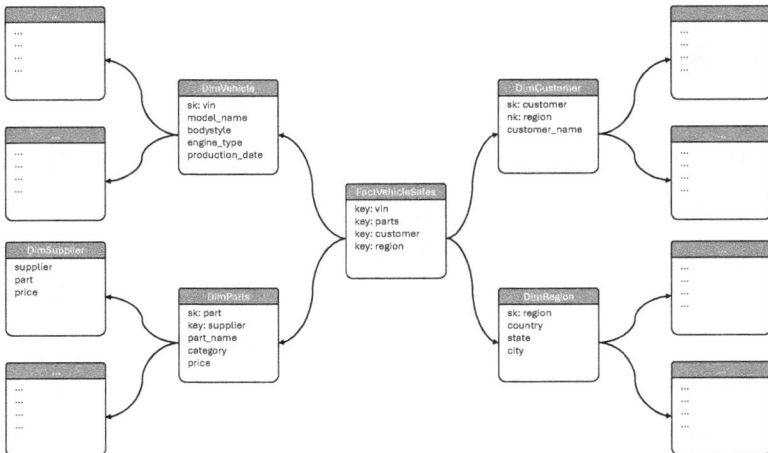

Figure 19: Snowflake example.

What differentiates the Snowflake schema from the Star schema is the additional level of normalization. In this case, we introduce a dimension under the parts dimension: the supplier. Each supplier delivers specific components, such as a door handle or a steering wheel. Depending on criteria like price or quality, we might source a part from Supplier A or Supplier B.

In a Star schema, supplier information would be embedded directly within the DimParts table. This could lead to duplication, where Supplier A and B appear multiple times. This increases the risk of inconsistencies. In contrast, the Snowflake schema separates suppliers into their own dimension table, improving consistency. However, this comes at the cost of increased query complexity and reduced ease of use.

Modeling strategies

Now we have a solid basis for modeling data based on some concrete techniques. There are several industry standards that build on the previously described concepts. We will briefly discuss these standards and their benefits and trade-offs.

Dimensional modeling

A widely used modeling technique is dimensional modeling, introduced by Ralph Kimball. It is often referred to as Kimball modeling. The core idea is to model data around business processes. It is based on the principle that if you understand the business, you can anticipate the types of queries that will be run. This reduces complexity and makes the data easier to use.

Dimensional modeling builds on the concepts of facts and dimensions, as seen in the Star and Snowflake schemas. Its goal is to strike a balance between query performance and ease of use. While normalization is still applied in the Snowflake variant, the focus is on the business view, not the system structure from which the data originates. Because it aligns well with how businesses think, dimensional modeling is often used in the Gold layer of the Medallion architecture. Although originally developed for traditional data warehouses, it is also well-suited for modern, cloud-based systems, including file-based architectures such as data lakes and lakehouses.

Data vault

Another key modeling technique is Data Vault. It is commonly used in complex enterprise environments and is particularly well-suited for historical tracking and auditability. One of its main advantages is its flexibility in changing environments, which makes it especially popular in large organizations.

Unlike Star or Snowflake schemas, Data Vault is based on three core components:

Hubs represent core business entities. In a car company, for example, a Hub could store Cars (with a VIN—Vehicle

Identification Number) or Customers (with a Customer ID). A Hub only stores identifiers and not descriptive data.

Links connect Hubs to capture relationships between entities. If a car (VIN) is sold to a customer (Customer ID), this relationship would be stored in a Link, defining which car was purchased by which customer.

Satellites contain the descriptive information about entities. For example, a Satellite for Cars might include car type, paint color, and powertrain; a Satellite for Customers might include address, email, or phone number. Satellites are historized, allowing you to track changes over time and build complex analytical models.

When to use which modeling strategy

In this table, we compare the different modeling techniques and when to use which:

	3NF	Dimensional	Data vault
Easy of use for businesses	Medium	High	Medium
Analytical performance	Low	High	Medium
Operational performance	High	Low	Low
Flexibility / schema evolution	Low	Medium	High

Ultimately, the choice of modeling strategy depends on the specific enterprise scenario. However, a best-of-breed approach works well when combined with the Medallion architecture. A recommended flow would look like this:

- **Bronze Layer**: Since this layer stays close to the source systems, we accept the data as it comes in. In many cases, this will be in Third Normal Form (3NF), as source systems focus on operational performance. Also, a lot of data will come to this layer in an unstructured format. This is especially the case for log data.

- **Silver Layer**: This layer introduces business logic but should remain flexible. Both dimensional modeling and Data Vault are suitable here. However, Data Vault often has an edge due to its flexibility and built-in support for history tracking.

- **Gold Layer:** This layer is focused on usability and business logic within the Data Product. Dimensional modeling is the preferred choice here, as it aligns closely with business processes and is easy for end users to work with.

A few words on technologies

This book does not aim to provide detailed descriptions of the technologies used for implementation. Instead, the focus is on the flow that Data Products go through. Still, it is important to briefly highlight the key technologies that support transformations between the layers of the Medallion architecture.

As mentioned in the previous chapter, Directed Acyclic Graphs (DAGs) play a crucial role in managing dependencies when moving data from Bronze to Silver and Gold. Tools like Apache Airflow or Dagster are commonly used for this purpose.

A major effort lies in the data transformations themselves. While DAGs control the execution order, other tools handle the logic of the transformation. Most cloud platforms offer their own solutions for this, but a common foundation across many tools is SQL. While SQL is not a tool in itself, it is used by many technologies, such as relational databases (PostgreSQL, Oracle, Microsoft SQL Server, Snowflake), Big Data frameworks like Apache Spark, and transformation frameworks like dbt.

This section is meant to provide a starting point for exploring these tools and concepts. For deep dives into individual technologies, there are dedicated books and resources available.[4]

Ensuring data quality in the integration phase

A Data Product is nothing without data quality. In this phase, there are several qualitative considerations we need to address.

---

[4] *The SQL Guide: From Fundamentals to Advanced*, by Ari Hovi, is a great reference to learn more about SQL.

Getting the data models right is one part, but equally important are the non-technical and non-modeling aspects that influence quality.

Let's begin by exploring those aspects.

Distributed data ownership

The first question is: who is ultimately responsible when data issues arise? As discussed earlier, those working directly with the data usually have the best understanding of its meaning and quality. They know when data is correct and when it isn't. This leads us to the concept of distributed data ownership.

There is no single person responsible for all data across the organization. While data models are often created by centralized teams, business representatives should be actively involved in the modeling process and ideally, have the final say on the structure of the model for their domain (though not necessarily on the technical implementation).

In practice, data is typically divided into domains, each with a corresponding data owner. For example, Marketing and Sales might own customer data, while Finance is responsible for financial data. Ownership is usually assigned at a senior level (e.g., Vice President or Director), although the operational responsibilities are handled by their teams.

Business glossary

A common challenge in many organizations is that different departments define and calculate the same KPI differently. This leads to conflicting reports and confusion about which numbers are correct. A key element in data governance that helps resolve this issue is the business glossary.

A business glossary is a centralized collection of agreed-upon definitions for business terms and KPIs. It ensures that everyone in the organization speaks the same language when it comes to metrics. Whether it's "customer churn," "revenue," or "active users." By aligning on definitions and calculation logic, a business glossary prevents conflicting interpretations and fosters consistency across teams.

Today, business glossaries are often integrated into modern data catalogs, making them easily accessible and part of the broader governance framework.

Data governance board

Not everything can be solved through a purely distributed setup. When conflicts arise, especially around key KPIs or overlapping data domains, there must be a central entity to resolve them. This is the role of the Data Governance Board.

The Data Governance Board is a formal group that typically includes data owners, data stewards, architects, and the person responsible for the overall data strategy. This is usually the Chief Data Officer (CDO). This board is tasked with harmonizing data assets, resolving ownership or definition conflicts, and ensuring that Data Products are built on consistent, high-quality data.

The board has a clear mandate: to oversee data quality and governance across the organization. Its decisions directly impact the structure and content of Data Products, reflected in data models, business glossaries, and metadata. The Data Governance Board ensures that governance is not just a policy but a living practice embedded in the way data is modeled, accessed, and used.

Master data and reference data management

A key challenge for ensuring quality in Data Products is proper Master Data and Reference Data Management. While we previously discussed metadata management, this section focuses specifically on these two related but distinct concepts.

Master Data refers to the core data entities in our data model that should be unique and consistent across systems. These are often called "Golden Records." The goal of Master Data Management (MDM) is to harmonize these key records across all systems and datasets. Take a customer, for example: in real life, "Mario Meir-Huber" (both Meir and Huber are the two most frequent last names in German speaking countries but this is the most uncommon pattern – connecting them via a hyphen; also, Mario is not a frequent last name in German speaking countries – so we can safely assume it is a unique person) is a single person. In our data, this individual should also appear only once, regardless of the system. However, in many enterprise environments, this isn't the case. A CRM system might store customers differently from the customer service system, resulting in duplicate or conflicting records. MDM addresses this issue for the most critical domains, ensuring consistency and reducing redundancy.

Reference data, on the other hand, includes standardized values such as country codes, zip codes, currencies, and other lookup values. While often seen as a byproduct of data management that is used frequently in joins and filters, it plays a crucial role in maintaining consistency across systems. Reference data differs from Master Data in function but is equally important for ensuring data integrity in analytical and operational workflows.

Key learnings

- **The flow of data**: How data flows through different layers, outlined with the medallion architecture.
- **Star and snowflake schema**: Elements of data modeling.
- **Different modeling approaches**: 3NF, dimensional modeling, and Data Vault.
- **Ensuring Quality in Data Modeling**: the Data Governance Board, distributed data ownership, and reference and master data management for the data integration part of a Data Product.

EIGHT

Extraction

Self-service reporting was a commodity in our organization, like in most modern companies. We had built numerous business-focused reports over the years, and usage was high. Teams relied on them daily: to track performance, measure the impact of sales campaigns, and see how call-center utilization shifted over the month and why.

Turning off the reporting service? No one considered it. Neither did I. The renewal was a month away, the budget secured and baked into our three-year forecast, all approved by the CFO's office. One final sign-off was still pending.

I met with the CFO, notes in hand outlining the BI renewal. He told me everything was fine and mentioned that a close relative of his held a senior role at the vendor.

Then everything changed. His relative was let go in a restructuring. The CFO's tone hardened; he began attacking the vendor and refused to approve the renewal workflow. We had one week left. Without renewal, the provider would shut us down. This would leave every business unit dark. No reports. No insight. A setback against our competitors. I sent impact analyses, emails, and explanations. Over and over again. He wouldn't listen. Emotion overrode pragmatism, with company-wide consequences. As other departments and board members became aware, the pressure mounted. On the very last day of the deadline, he approved. We avoided interruption.

This story sets up the themes of this chapter. First, the people side of Data Products: emotions, resistance, and change management needed to bring stakeholders on board.[5] People don't always react with pragmatism, as shown in the story above. Then, we pivot towards value extraction: self-service reporting is one path, but there are many others we'll explore next.

Change management: shifting the mindset of an organization for better data utilization

As the opening story illustrates, people aren't machines and they don't always act pragmatically. Change is often perceived as a

---

[5] *Humanizing Data Strategy*, by Tiankai Feng does a fantastic job covering the people side.

threat. A small group embraces it early, many wait and watch, and a sizable group resists.

That resistance is not a flaw; it's human. Caution toward sudden shifts once helped us survive changing environments. The instinct persists: when something new appears, pushing back can feel safer than leaning in.

Data Products are no exception. A new dashboard? "Why not keep the old one?" A new API? "The current one works." An AI model? "This will never fly." These reactions are common and predictable.

There are many drivers of resistance. One is fear of not understanding. People worry about looking uninformed, so they avoid the new and cling to the familiar. Effective change management meets them where they are: lower the barrier to entry, make learning safe, and offer clear, hands-on guidance.

Another challenge is ownership: taking responsibility makes teams feel vulnerable. This is especially difficult with distributed domain ownership. All of a sudden, a business unit is accountable for data. That shift often creates friction; teams may want the data but not the ownership. Effective stakeholder management is critical to success.

In the next sections, we'll focus on practical ways to support that journey and bring stakeholders on board.

Communicating the change

A key aspect of managing change is clear communication. This typically involves working closely with HR, as they often have dedicated professionals trained to craft messages that help people understand and accept change. When the transformation is more substantial, a dedicated communication plan becomes essential.

Every communication should start by answering the "why" behind the change. When introducing a new Data Product, explaining why it's being introduced must come before explaining what it is. This principle is well captured in Simon Sinek's "Start with Why", a book I highly recommend to anyone working in technology or change-driven environments.

The "why" message is critical. If people don't understand the purpose behind the new Data Product, they won't be interested in the details. Once the "why" is clear and has captured attention, we can move on to explain what the Data Product does and how it does it.

Let's revisit the call-center example from earlier in the book. The call center was running blind on call reasons; without that information, improvement wasn't possible. The Why is to make the lives of call-center agents easier. We can frame the Data Product like this: "We're introducing the Call-Center Data Product to reduce agent workload and improve work-life balance, while lowering costs." This is a powerful why: it speaks to a meaningful benefit for people and delivers savings. Once attention is earned, explain what it does and how.

Learning programs

Resistance can be significantly reduced when people understand the new Data Product. This has two key benefits: first, users will apply it more effectively; second, hands-on experience lowers emotional resistance.

Two proven approaches help here:

1. Role-focused learning paths, tailored to specific needs.
2. Short, snackable learning videos, inspired by formats on platforms like TikTok.

Let's start with tailored learning paths. These are typically developed in collaboration with HR. The idea is to identify key roles in the organization and design training paths specifically for them. Some roles require deep expertise, while others just need the essentials. For instance, a data scientist in Marketing needs detailed guidance on how to work with the Data Product. A Director or VP, by contrast, may only need a high-level understanding.

Learning paths are usually delivered as blended formats: some roles benefit from in-person workshops, others can be trained entirely online. Many companies also integrate external platforms like LinkedIn Learning to supplement internal content and accelerate rollout.

The second approach is based on short videos. I like to call them "DataTok". This is a clear nod to TikTok that instantly sets expectations: short, engaging, and focused.

Short-form videos help capture attention and lower the barrier to trying a new Data Product. Platforms like TikTok have changed how people consume content. Today, users expect condensed information in seconds, not minutes. Of course, complex topics can't be fully explained in ten seconds, so each video should focus on a very specific task. For example: "See your customer lifetime value in 90 seconds". This is done in a short, focused walkthrough that shows exactly how to access and interpret a key dashboard.

To make these videos effective within their condensed format, several principles are important:

- **Stay focused**: Each video should address one specific question or use case and nothing more.
- **Keep it brief:** Aim for a runtime that fits into short attention spans and busy schedules. These videos should feel effortless to watch in short breaks.
- **Be demonstrative**: Avoid slides and show the actual Data Product in use. Let viewers see how it works in practice.
- **Include a clear call to action**: End with something actionable, like "Open the dashboard and try it yourself."

Feedback channels

Things change significantly when people are given a platform to express their needs and concerns openly. During a large-scale transformation I led, I introduced regular feedback sessions. These were open-door formats where employees could raise questions or voice worries directly.

These sessions were initially held twice a week, later scaled down to weekly, and after two months, we were able to phase them out as concerns subsided. Early on, participation was high. We implemented some of the feedback directly; others we couldn't. When we could not implement it, we always explained why we were not going for it to the leadership team. Simply rejecting an idea without context leads to frustration. Transparent communication matters, even when the answer is no.

In parallel, I maintained a steady stream of updates in our Teams channel. A format I introduced was called "Week in Review". This is a short post summarizing developments, decisions, and the thinking behind them. The format helped everyone stay aligned and gave people a consistent place to find updates and understand the bigger picture. I posted that every Friday morning to summarize the week for the teams.

Having a clear, trusted "go-to" channel for feedback and updates is critical. It not only builds transparency, but it also builds trust.

Communities and change ambassadors

When introducing Data Products on a continuous basis, it's important to create structures within the business units most affected by these changes. In every organization, there is always a small group of people who naturally embrace change. While they're a minority, they can become the foundation for broader adoption.

These individuals can be gradually involved as the rollout unfolds. We often refer to them as change ambassadors. They're embedded in remote or decentralized units and play a crucial role in reaching parts of the organization that are otherwise difficult to engage. Their influence is informal but powerful: they talk to their peers during coffee breaks, at lunch, and at company events. This helps reduce resistance and build trust from within.

Because these ambassadors are distributed across the organization, they should be connected through a community. This creates a structured way to involve them, share updates, and build momentum. Through this community, change ambassadors stay informed about important developments and gain a platform to connect with like-minded colleagues across other units.

Engaging people who are "on your side" from the beginning is a critical step in building a data-driven culture. It strengthens the adoption of Data Products and should be a core element of every Data Product program from day one on.

Democratizing Data Product Access

A core goal of every Data Product is democratized access. This only works when access is highly automated and the practices from previous chapters are in place. The enterprise data catalog is the front door: it makes Data Products discoverable and requestable. Importantly, accessibility is not a single step as it spans the entire lifecycle of a Data Product.

Democratizing access is not just a technical exercise. It does require mechanisms like RBAC and access policies, but it is primarily an organizational topic. The company must define what "access" means, who should have it, and how to implement it lawfully. Regional regulations differ and may conflict. For example, the EU's GDPR emphasizes data minimization and purpose limitation, often operationalized as a "need-to-know" approach. To enable access to Data Products, establish a clear policy and execution model first. Technology is only the enabler.

Access strategies for Data Products: BI, AI, APIs, and data spaces

As defined throughout the book, a Data Product is always end-to-end. And by exposing these Data Products, we have now reached the state of having the lifecycle complete. This last section of this volume is all about one thing: putting the paint onto the car. Everything is engineered, prepared, and ready to be consumed.

But how can a Data Product be consumed? There are different strategies, and we will now elaborate on them in this section.

A key thing to consider is that even though there are different appearances described, we always keep talking about Data Products – even though the representation is finally done by BI, AI, or any other form. There are some streams that define them differently, such as an "AI Product" or "Analytical Product". Let's elaborate a bit on this topic and use the metaphor of our cars one last time. A car is a car and stays a car. However, there might be different types of cars, such as convertibles, SUVs, pickups, or limousines. The same holds true for our Data Products. When they are exposed as AI, they might be called "AI Product". But eventually, AI is built on data—a lot of data. A convertible car still stays a car in essence, and this is how we treat it in the book. Both terms (AI Product and Data Product) are right in their very own sense, but an AI Product is built on a Data Product. How you call it is up to you. If you build your Data Products with quality in mind, naming doesn't matter.

Now let's have a look at different access strategies and what it needs for them to succeed.

Reporting and business intelligence

Business Intelligence (BI) is the most common way to access Data Products in enterprises. BI makes Data Products broadly consumable through focused reports and dashboards. Because speed matters, BI typically pairs with denormalized schemas to minimize joins and improve query performance. Self-service reporting is now a commodity, with many tools available, and we won't elaborate in this book on concrete BI tools.

Self-service only works if upstream steps are done well with clear models, validated data, and complete metadata:

Ambiguity or missing metadata quickly limits what business teams can do on their own.

However, enterprise-grade BI is not the only way a Data Product can create value. Consider Google Analytics: a widely used product built on large volumes of data and exposed through dashboards. Many standalone Data Products present value in a similar way: feature-rich, user-facing dashboards (including those built with open-source tools). In all cases, the underlying data should flow through the processes described earlier in the book to ensure quality and integrity. And because users expect responsiveness, fast read performance remains essential, again favoring denormalized data for superior read speeds.

API

Imagine we've built dashboards in Google Analytics to track customer behavior on our website. One day, the marketing director asks if this data can be integrated into a churn prediction algorithm. For example, if a user frequently visits the "How to cancel my contract" page, that behavior could be a strong indicator of churn. This insight would be incredibly valuable for the algorithm. Fortunately, APIs (short for Application Programming Interfaces) make this possible. APIs allow systems to exchange data in a structured way. In this case, an API lets us extract the relevant web behavior data from Google Analytics and feed it into our predictive model.

APIs are a powerful enabler of Data Product value creation. They allow seamless integration of Data Products into other systems. Be it applications, machine learning models, or dashboards. Most APIs are built as RESTful web services, and well-designed ones are also packaged into libraries for popular programming languages like Python, Java, or.NET.

While dashboards target business users, APIs target a more technical audience, such as software engineers and system integrators. APIs are rarely standalone; rather, they are often exposed as an extension of an existing Data Product, enabling deeper integration and automation. In the case of Google Analytics, the dashboard is just one way to consume the product and the API is another, opening the door to custom applications, algorithms, and use cases.

Analytics and Artificial Intelligence (AI)

Let's revisit our churn algorithm example: We want to identify customers likely to cancel their contracts, based on their behavior, such as frequently visiting a "How to cancel my contract" page. To do this, we need large volumes of granular data about user interactions. This kind of use case is a perfect example of analytics-driven value creation in Data Products.

While Business Intelligence (BI) focuses on providing a snapshot of the current situation, Analytics is about looking forward. It uses historical data to predict future behavior. Unlike dashboards, which rely on highly aggregated and denormalized data for speed, analytics thrives on detailed, raw, or semi-transformed data.

Analytics pipelines often feed into machine learning models that drive decision-making, like identifying high-risk customers. These models may surface through reports, be exposed via APIs, or even be embedded into consumer-facing apps or operational systems. This makes analytics a critical, behind-the-scenes engine for value extraction.

Closely related to analytics is the field of Artificial Intelligence (AI). While AI is a broader discipline within Data Science, often associated with techniques like deep learning, we focus here on the language-based side of AI. Large Language Models (LLMs) such as OpenAI's ChatGPT have become widely recognized and are often used synonymously with AI in public discourse. For our purposes, we treat them as interfaces to expose Data Products for broader, conversational use.

There are several ways to integrate LLMs with Data Products. The first method we look at is through the Model Context Protocol

(MCP), a protocol designed to enable seamless communication between LLMs and external services. By implementing MCP, a Data Product can securely and consistently expose its content or functions to an LLM, making it accessible via natural language queries. A MCP Server consists of tools, resources, and prompts.

Let's revisit our earlier example of customer churn to explain how the Model Context Protocol (MCP) works in practice. In this scenario, a tool might return a list of customers with a churn probability of "High" or "Very High." Tools in MCP are dynamic components. When the LLM calls a tool, it executes code in the background. Another tool in this context could be one that calculates the churn probability for a specific customer based on current data. These tools allow the LLM to perform live computations and interact with the underlying logic of a Data Product. In contrast, a resource is static, and they are read-only for the LLM. It provides data and does not trigger any computation. Using the same example, a resource could be a customer profile that includes contact details, region, or historical behavior, which is useful context for further analysis but not dynamically generated.

The third element in MCP is the prompt. Prompts are pre-defined instructions or templates that guide the LLM in how to interact with tools and resources. For example, a prompt might define how to ask for churn data, how to interpret it, and how to phrase responses back to the user. Figure 20 illustrates how tools and resources are used in an MCP-based integration.

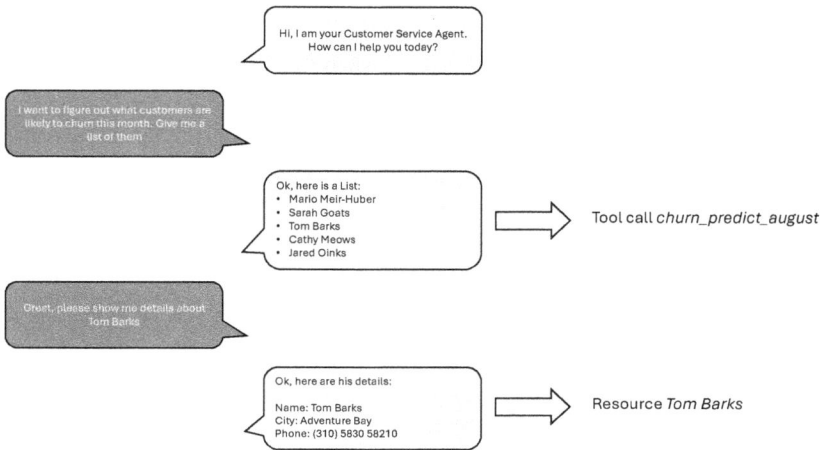

Figure 20: How tools and resources are used in an MCP-based integration.

As illustrated in the figure, the interaction begins with the LLM calling a tool that calculates churn risk for customers in the month of August. This function executes a data science algorithm embedded within our Data Product. In the next step, a customer service representative asks for information about a specific customer: "Tom Barks." The LLM then retrieves this data as a resource from the MCP server, since it is a static, read-only element.

Another advanced method to expose Data Products is through vectorization. This involves converting text or structured data into a numerical format that LLMs can interpret. Vectorization is particularly useful when training LLMs with highly domain-specific knowledge, especially when the data is too niche to be part of a general model's training corpus. However, it's important to note that this approach is more complex and less suited for fast-changing or dynamic datasets. Vectorized data is better used in static or specialized scenarios, such as enriching an LLM with domain-specific terminology or documentation.

Data spaces

Many Data Products are not created in isolation within a single organization; they span across company boundaries. Take the automotive industry, for example. Modern cars are assembled from components sourced from various suppliers: one company manufactures the seats, another provides the tires, and yet another handles the infotainment system. This highly distributed production process also creates a complex data landscape.

This is where Data Spaces come into play. Data Spaces offer a standardized, interoperable environment that allows multiple organizations to share data securely and in a sovereign manner. In our car example, the seat manufacturer retains full control over its data but can grant the car manufacturer selective access, all without losing ownership. If the partnership ends, the data flow stops. This setup creates a trusted collaboration environment where companies can exchange valuable data without compromising control.

Let's consider another real-world example to visualize the impact of Data Spaces. This time from the ESG (Environmental, Social, and Governance) domain. Since I'm Austrian, I'll take skiing as a reference. Skiing is deeply embedded in Austrian culture, but it's also extremely energy-intensive. Ski lifts consume vast amounts of power, hotels in alpine regions require constant heating, and artificial snow machines run around the clock.

In a recent initiative, hotels in a ski region began sharing their booking forecasts via a Data Space. This allowed ski lift operators to anticipate guest volumes and adjust their lift schedules accordingly: slowing them down during low occupancy periods to reduce energy consumption. This operational data was also shared with energy providers, who could then optimize electricity production days in advance, leading to a more sustainable energy footprint for the entire region.

The key enabler for Data Spaces is trust. When multiple parties exchange data, trust becomes non-negotiable. And this is exactly where Data Products make the difference: they embed quality, transparency, and clearly defined ownership, making them the ideal unit of exchange in Data Spaces.

Extracting the value

There is no single path that leads to value extraction in a Data Product. The same churn product can inform an executive dashboard, surface through an API into POS workflows, support service agents via conversational assistants, or be shared with partners in a Data Space. In each case, we are working with one core asset expressed through different interfaces, meeting users where their work happens and allowing value to emerge in context. Data Products can thus be described as polymorphic in how they surface.

Extracting the value is key to success in Data Products. If we look at Data Products without these aspects and say "A Dashboard isn't part of a Data Product," we fully ignore the business dimension of Data Products, and they remain technical solutions. They don't differ from traditional topics we saw in the past. Data Products are end-to-end, and the value extraction is a core ingredient to them.

Throughout the book, we learned about the GAP in Data Products. Governance gives us clarity, accountability, trust, and compliance; Architecture provides the runway for a solid technical foundation, reliable delivery, and evolution; People is the non-technical aspect relevant for our Data Products.

When these elements move in step, we find that technical excellence and business value reinforce each other rather than compete. To achieve that, we learned about the framework that ensures business value and technical feasibility.

Data Products are more than technology; they create value when we see them in the wider context of people, decisions, and outcomes. Data is never still, and neither are we. The work is demanding, and failure is part of the craft, yet with each iteration we learn, simplify, and move closer to excellence. The intent of this book is to make that journey lighter, helping us sidestep familiar pitfalls and giving us the language, practices, and confidence to build Data Products that matter.

Index

www.ingramcontent.com/pod-product-compliance
Lightning Source LLC
Chambersburg PA
CBHW071602210326
41597CB00019B/3373